ANNIE DAVY

A SENSE OF PLACE

Mindful practice outdoors

FEATHERSTONE

FEATHERSTONE
Bloomsbury Publishing Plc
50 Bedford Square, London, WC1B 3DP, UK

BLOOMSBURY, FEATHERSTONE and the Feather logo are trademarks of Bloomsbury Publishing Plc

First published in Great Britain, 2019 by Bloomsbury Publishing Plc

Photographs © Shutterstock: pp. 10, 11, 13, 15 (sundial), 16 (backpack), 19 (sticks), 20 (pens), 23, 24, 26 (fairy door), 27 (pebbles), 28 (trowel), 32 (snail and magnifier), 34, 38, 40, 41 (children running and sunflowers), 42 (children), 44 (pine cone), 46 (peas), 48 (boy with log), 53 (wasp), 55, 59 (boats), 63, 68 (girl with potato), 70, 72, 73, 76, 78, 79 (child in orange top), 80, 82, 83, 88 (butterfly), 92, 94, 96, 98, 100 (nature pics), 101, 102, 105 (elderberries), 106 (pebbles), 110 and 111, and all illustrations. Annie Davy: pp. 21 (teacher with boy sunflower), 43, 44, 64, 81. Pippa Hamwee: pp. 8, 15 (girl in tree), 57, 64 (girl in leaves), 88 (girl with geese), 89. Hilary Kneale: pp. 64 (feet). Lazaar: pp. 42 (wheelbarrow planter). Rose Macaffee: pp. 29 (boy crawling in water), 46 (ice eating), 50 (boy in snow). Kay Gatehouse, Schnell Photography: all other photos.

A catalogue record for this book is available from the British Library

ISBN: PB: 978-1-4729-5365-0; ePDF: 978-1-4729-5366-7; ePub: 978-1-4729-5367-4

2 4 6 8 10 9 7 5 3

Text design by Lynda Murray

Printed and bound in India by Replika Press Pvt. Ltd.

FSC
www.fsc.org

MIX
Paper from
responsible sources
FSC® C016779

All papers used by Bloomsbury Publishing Plc are natural, recyclable products from wood grown in well managed forests. The manufacturing processes conform to the environmental regulations of the country of origin

To find out more about our authors and books visit www.bloomsbury.com and sign up for our newsletters

Acknowledgments
With deep gratitude and appreciation to my teachers of mindfulness and nature connection and my many companions in learning about our beautiful Earth. Thanks to all at Grandpont Nursery School for their help with this book. Thanks to Lynda Murray for the design and layout. Thank you to my daughters Loren, Gemma and Ella who have taught me more about life than they can possibly yet know.

Contents

Part 1 — Setting the scene – landscapes for learning in a changing world

Chapter 1: Changing lives, changing landscapes

Chapter 2: A place to play – learning with the landscape

 *Doorways, windows, skylights – learning through the senses*

Chapter 3: Sense doorways – sight, sound, touch, smell and taste

Chapter 4: Sense windows – survival, wellbeing, independence, meaning

Chapter 5: Sense skylights – values for a living world

A sense of place

 *A sense of place – mindfulness, resilience and community*

Chapter 6: Mindfulness pedagogy in the Early Years

Chapter 7: Roots of resilience – a systemic approach

Chapter 8: Nature pedagogy, community, and conscious action

References and further reading

Author preface

> 'To be alive in this beautiful, self-organizing universe – to participate in the dance of life with senses to perceive it, lungs that breathe it, organs that draw nourishment from it – is a wonder beyond words.'
>
> Joanna Macy

It doesn't need much in terms of material 'stuff' to ignite children's capacity to learn, but it needs your everything to 'tend the flame' and build a fire in the hearts and minds of young children – a resilient fire of enthusiasm for learning and confidence to have a go. It needs your undivided attention and ability to be fully present – knowing when to step forward to help or support and when to step back. As teachers and carers of young children, it takes sensitivity and skill to know when to speak and when to share the silence, when to move and when to be still. Noticing what is happening in nature each moment and each day throughout the year is excellent training in observation. By learning from direct experience with nature, you and the children will develop in all areas of learning – maths, art, science, language – in a very real and practical way.

My wish for you, in your work with young children, in your explorations and shared learning journeys outdoors, is that you will see the potential for awe and wonder, curiosity and engagement at every turn. I hope you will have the time and space to 'just be' as well as 'do', to feel a sense of peace and wellbeing in your work.

Annie Davy

Early development of ecological literacy

Introduction

> 'The universe is full of magical things, patiently waiting for our wits to grow sharper.'
>
> Eden Phillpotts

About this book

Every child needs attentive, discerning carers and teachers to help them to learn and develop the skills and dispositions they need to survive and thrive. They need the best possible conditions to develop resilience in a rapidly changing world. This book is for anyone caring for or teaching children in their earliest years. It is about spending time outdoors and working with nature as a resource and source for teaching, learning and understanding children and ourselves better. It offers a holistic view of child development and learning through the senses – how young children learn to perceive themselves, others and the world around them.

The book is firmly grounded in the real experience of a great many Early Years' practitioners, as well as parents, grandparents and carers. It has been inspired by their questions and their insights into the challenges and opportunities of caring for and teaching young children in our times. It draws on research and learning from biophysical sciences, neuroscience, psychology and deep ecology.

Ecological identity and Earth-mindedness

Your identity is who you are, the way you think about yourself, the way you are viewed by the world and the characteristics that define you. Your ecological identity is how you think of yourself as a biological being – as part of a wider ecological system, as part of nature rather than separate from it. It is formed by your awareness and acceptance of your impermanence, and how you embrace birth, life and death. It is your understanding of your interdependence with the living world of plants and other animals. Your ecological identity is more than just knowing all this as scientific 'fact' – it is your sense of who you are and how comfortable you are in your skin.

One of the purposes of this book is to support teachers and carers to develop a balanced curriculum which positively supports children's ecological identity. Many of us have become distanced from ecological identities – living in cities, in centrally-heated homes and eating processed

food – maybe preferring to see ourselves as separate from nature and in control of it. This identity separation creates a schism in our thinking that enables us to behave as over-consumers and exploiters of nature's resources, often against the interests of both our individual and collective health and wellbeing. This will be a recurring theme throughout the book.

There are other key themes or golden threads running through all the chapters in this book:

- ✿ the importance of children's early years and each child's unique journey in the context of the outdoors

- ✿ a holistic framework for understanding child development and perception through the senses (sense doorways and windows)

- ✿ the importance of talking about and sharing our values (sense skylights) and aligning our behaviour towards ourselves, others and the wider living world in practical ways

- ✿ resources for developing resilience to help children navigate the complexities and uncertainties of our times

- ✿ mindfulness practices to help you slow down and be more present when working with young children

- ✿ nature as the fundamental resource for young children's learning and wellbeing; ecological literacy as part the young child's natural curriculum.

Nature is a fundamental resource for wellbeing and learning

Structure of the book

The book is structured in three parts.

Outside space to explore

Setting the scene – landscapes for learning in a changing world

Chapter 1 is about the context for work with young children outdoors, and why working outdoors is more important than ever in our digital age. It invites you to reflect on your own learning journey and how this affects the way you work.

Chapter 2 gives some theoretical and practical perspectives on working with nature and outdoors and offers advice for how to develop learning environments and places where children can flourish.

Doorways, windows, skylights – learning through the senses

Part 2 offers a model of childhood perceptual development based on three different ways that children 'sense' themselves, others and the world around them:

- ✿ Sense doorways: sight, hearing, touch, taste and smell
- ✿ Sense windows: survival, wellbeing, independence and meaning
- ✿ Sense skylights: kindness, equality, fairness, freedom

Chapter 3 describes the five sense doorways of sight, hearing, touch, taste and smell. The sense doorways enable young children to explore, understand and manipulate the materials of the world. Simply being in nature, outside and under the sky, helps the sense doorways to open. As teachers and carers, we can support sensory-based learning by offering a rich variety of materials, tastes, sounds, smells, textures. We can give children experience of all elements of the outdoors – water, earth, air, wood, stone, metal, plants and animals.

Chapter 4 is about the sense windows. These are: survival, wellbeing, independence and meaning. The sense windows are subtler than sense doorways; they are less about children 'taking in' the external world, and more about how they develop their internal responses to it. The survival window includes the senses of temperature, hunger and pain. The window of wellbeing includes vitality, emotional stability, engagement and flow. The independence window includes balance, movement and orientation. The window of meaning includes the deep structures of thought, feeling, language and expression. Working outdoors and with nature expands the opportunities for all these senses. You can also use the sense windows to notice what children need to support their development.

Chapter 5 is about the sense skylights, which are essentially our values towards the living world. Going beyond the 'British values' prescribed in the English national curriculum and Early Years Foundation Stage, this chapter looks at four core values: kindness, equality, fairness and freedom. From a very early age, children pick up our values through the language and behaviour we use towards each other and towards the environment. They learn about what we value and what we disregard through the things we include and make important and the things we ignore. Working outside with nature provides an endless number of opportunities to demonstrate the values of earth-mindedness. You can model the sense skylights in the ways in which you care for and behave towards the children, yourself, other people and the wider living world.

- • Sight
- • Hearing
- • Touch
- • Taste
- • Smell

- • Survival
- • Wellbeing
- • Independence
- • Meaning

- • Kindness
- • Equality
- • Fairness
- • Freedom

A sense of place

A sense of place – mindfulness, resilience and community

Part 3 offers some systemic approaches to working with children by developing mindfulness, building resilience and drawing on the resources of community, culture and conscious action.

Chapter 6 is an introduction to mindfulness pedagogy in the Early Years. Research shows that practising mindfulness can help people of all ages to build their physical and mental resilience in their busy and often complex lives. Mindfulness is something we may have naturally, but that can also be developed with regular practice. It is an art and a skill, a way of thinking and a way of being.

Chapter 7 explores some routes to resilience including maps to support your thinking about your own resilience and the resilience of the children in your setting. Resilience enables us to face the challenges of life and bounce back after difficulties, to recognise what we can change for the better and to do something about it.

Chapter 8 is about nature pedagogy, community and conscious action. As teachers and carers, our work with children takes place in a wider context. It has a geographical place or neighbourhood and a community of parents and carers, colleagues and other agencies involved in the lives of our children. This chapter explores ways in which we can develop a shared sense of place and a connection with the wider community. It suggests that those who teach young children have a responsibility to care for the environment that supports them because it is their inheritance.

A shared sense of place

Mindfulness is a way of being

The structure of each chapter

Each chapter has:

❀ Key ideas that will be introduced in the chapter.

❀ On reflection exercises, which can often be completed individually but are most useful when discussed with other practitioners.

❀ In practice sections, which offer ideas for projects or ways of working with children outdoors.

❀ Narratives, which are case studies or learning journeys that illustrate a point.

There is a further reading section at the end of each chapter to help you extend your learning.

On reflection

Each chapter in this book contains 'on reflection' sections – invitations for you that offer food for thought and reflections to support you. These sections contain powerful questions and suggested exercises to assist your mindfulness practice, reflective awareness and develop your resilience in your work. You can use the 'on reflection' sections to develop your own ideas or simple personal practices. They can also be helpful if shared with a team or a group of peers at training sessions, team meetings or team development days.

In practice

These sections give practical ideas for working with children and with nature: ways of being, ways of doing, ideas for activities and ideas for being less 'busy' and more 'present'. These sections explore the resources you can gather for your work from the constantly changing elements of nature. There are practical ideas and photos in this book to inspire you to create environments, undertake activities or try new ways of working or simply 'being with' the children with greater awareness. These are ideas that have been tried by others and been found to be helpful in creating a greater sense of peace, wellbeing and enjoyment.

Narrative

Sometimes we learn best from hearing about the experiences of others. The narratives in this book are examples, case studies or learning journeys to illustrate the key concepts and ideas. Names have been changed but they are all drawn from real experience.

Inspirational quotes or poems

There are times when it is only through art or poetry that we can find ways to express the 'felt sense' of what we mean. I have been inspired by the current and recent poetry and writing of poets such Mary Oliver, Gary Snyder, Wendell Berry, David Whyte and many others. Whilst not being early childhood practitioners themselves, their words seem to express more deeply my sense of what a 'deep ecology' approach to early education can mean.

Collecting our own inspirations and quotes and putting them around our place of work can help 'lift' us out of our everyday routines and remind us why we do the work we do. There is no more important work than teaching young children; sharing with them the delights and discoveries of the world we live in.

Further reading

The ideas in this book have often been developed through reading articles, books and resources written by people I respect and who have gone before, as well as practical work with children and Early Years practitioners. This book will hopefully inspire you to find out more. Early education pedagogy, the philosophy and neuroscience behind mindfulness, Earth sciences and environmental activism, psychology and deep ecology all have strong and inspiring traditions and there is so much to read, learn and discover. There are suggestions for browsing the Internet and recommendations for further reading at the end of each chapter.

A sense of place

Changing lives, changing landscapes

'We don't see things as they are – we see them as we are.'

Original source unknown

Chapter overview

We live in a rapidly changing world. How does this affect the experiences of young children growing up? How does it impact their environments and relationships? As teachers, we need to respond to these changes and modify, flex and adapt the curriculum, environment and opportunities that we offer. This chapter encourages you to reflect on changes in your own life and your sense of place and connection with nature. Your past experiences shape the way you see the world now. Your children and their families have had their own unique journeys which shape their perspective and how they see things. The chapter raises questions about how you meet the challenges for children growing up in our time. It has suggestions for how you can support children's sense of place and belonging through developing an understanding of time and change and how these affect us and the wider living world.

Key ideas

- ✿ Human developments and challenges of our time

- ✿ A systemic and ecological view of child development

- ✿ Each child and adult's experience is unique

- ✿ Changes over time

- ✿ Understanding the system of culture, values and beliefs

- ✿ 'Nature deficit disorder' or a sense of place?

- ✿ Belonging to a place

Human developments and challenges of our time

Over the last 150 years, the age of industry has dramatically altered our landscapes and changed our communities worldwide. There has been increasing urbanisation as more and more people move from the countryside to work in cities. Over the last 25 years or so, the new era of technology and digitisation has also transformed the landscape, affecting the way we communicate, behave, learn and interact. We now have a world of data, information (and misinformation) accessible at our fingertips, in our homes and in the classroom. Technology has enabled us to create global networks, markets and communities of interest that we could not have imagined even thirty years ago. There are few, if any, places in the world that have not been impacted by human habitation or influence.

The age of technology and digitisation has transformed the landscape for most young children

A systemic and ecological view of child development

In their first few years from conception to seven, children learn more and faster than they will learn in the rest of their lives. During these vital years, with help from others around them, they create the groundwork for their future health, wellbeing, learning and development. They learn to move their bodies and develop skills for making, creating, writing and doing practical things which support their independence and survival. Their bodies learn to resist disease. Through their interactions with the world, neural pathways are formed in the body and brain, and connections are made between one experience and another. Children's minds are naturally curious to learn, and they have innate capacity to express themselves in ever more complex ways. They develop relationships with other people and the wider living world. They absorb culture and values and develop their own unique character. Although we continue to develop as humans throughout our lives, the foundations of body and mind will have been laid in the first few years.

The ecological model of child development developed by Urie Bronfenbrenner teaches us that we cannot separate the children from the context of their immediate environment and, beyond that, the wider community and the world. There is a constant interaction between the child and the widening 'systems' of his or her environment – each affecting the other to varying degrees from the earliest days of life.

The foundations of body and mind are laid in the first few years

An ecological model of child development
(Adapted from the work of Urie Bronfenbrenner)

A sense of place

Each child and adult's experience is unique

The children in your care may have already travelled widely. They may have moved from one country to another or moved from a different village, town or city, or they may have been born and lived around the corner from your setting for their whole lives. They may have local parents and grandparents, or ones that live far away, or who have migrated from another part of the world. They may have a garden or live in a high-rise flat with no access to outdoor space except a view of the sky. They may have carers at home who always take them to the park and who take them on holiday to wild places – beaches, forest, mountains. Or they may never have experienced any of these things.

On reflection

RIVER OF LIFE AND NATURE CONNECTION EXERCISE

1. Take 20 minutes to draw your life as a river and mark the key milestones in its course from your birth to the present day.

Think about these questions to help you create your river of life: Where were you born? What was your river's source? What have been the key landscapes and memories of play and learning as a child? Where were the curves in the river – such as changes in direction through moving home, changing school, going to college, changing jobs? Was your river joined by any tributaries – key relationships or other things that have influenced your life? When were the rapids of intense activity? Were there any wide-open pools of time – calm expanses when things were slower?

2. When your river is complete, it can be helpful to share it with someone you trust, such as a friend or a colleague. You might want to talk about:

- Who are the key people and what are the events and experiences that have influenced the course of your life so far?

- How did they influence your beliefs and values and the ways you work with children now?

- What were the key landscapes of your life and how did they shape your memories?

- Can you remember any sense of belonging or 'displacement' at various stages of your journey so far?

Changes over time

In Victorian times, the key paediatric concerns were child poverty, child labour and high rates of infant mortality. Many of these were caused by the demands of the Industrial Revolution along with the increase of urban developments without sanitation and clean water. Over one hundred years on, childhood mortality (those under four) is now rare in the UK, mainly due to improvements in environmental factors such as housing, medicine and sanitation. People gradually took control and learned to manage the new industrial technologies, but now there are increasing concerns about the rise of new morbidities, such as childhood obesity. There are also growing concerns about behavioural, attention and speech and language disorders. It cannot be coincidence that the rise in health issues and other concerns runs parallel to rapid developments and a new age of technology. We are still learning about the impacts of technology and how to manage them. Within one or two generations, life as we know it has changed considerably. Change happens on a personal level in our family or community and it happens socially and politically worldwide too. The past and present shape us and we cannot know what the future holds.

What were the landscapes of your childhood?

Narrative

TIME TRAVELLER TO THE AGE OF STUFF: AN IMAGINARY JOURNEY THROUGH TIME

Imagine a time traveller Early Years' practitioner from the 1980s arriving in a typical city in the UK in 2019. The first thing she notices is the increase in road traffic. Then she notices that the people are often apparently talking to themselves – or talking into little hand-held devices clutched to their ears; many others are wearing headsets. She sees no prams – babies are transported in lightweight buggies or lifted in car seats, often facing away from their carers and facing the onslaught of people, noise and traffic.

Our time traveller sees far fewer children out and about on their own in the parks, woods, playgrounds and streets. When she slips inside the houses, she starts with the kitchen. No sign of children – they are in front of the TV or playing with multiple plastic toys under the soundscape of the TV or music. She finds the older children in their bedrooms communicating 'virtually' with their schoolmates through something called social media or being entertained by any number of computer games or other screen-based devices.

She notices children and adults with their eyes glued to screens and ears blocked by mobile devices. She sees parents distracted by the volume of information and communication being poured their way – through emails and text alerts – all demanding instant attention and responses, or trying to sell them something. Children too are targeted with a stream of adverts aimed at them: have this toy, this game, this kind of clothing or equipment.

Our time traveller looks closer and marvels with genuine awe and wonder at the possibilities of new technology to push the boundaries of our learning and communication, enabling children, teachers and any individual to reach out across the world without ever having to take an aeroplane. She wonders why all this technology has apparently not freed up people's time for more play and leisure or for more time to access to the great outdoors. She wonders why so many people seem more anxious, hurried and harried. She is amazed and also confused by her brief glimpse into this new age of so much 'stuff'.

Spending time outside and observing nature gives us many opportunities to experience change and time in a tangible fashion that children can relate to: the sun rises and moves across the sky each day; plants grow from seedling to tall trees and flowers; the seasons mark the passage of the year. There are many ways in we can help children understand the dimensions of change over time as well as the recurring rhythms of nature.

Visit tall trees and find out how long they have been growing

A sense of place

Make a sundial and plot the length of shadows

In practice

TIME AND NATURE'S RHYTHMS

When working outside you will be more aware of the changes that happen over time – in the course of the day as the sun casts changing shadows, or in the course of each season or over a lifetime. If you work with nature, you can use nature's rhythms to influence your work and play. Here are a few suggestions:

1. Make a sundial and plot the length of shadows on sunny days throughout the year.

2. Work with the changes in seasons, following their rhythm, making your planning chime with what you notice outdoors (see Chapter 6).

3. Harvest and eat seasonal food. Cultivate a relationship with an allotment association or someone with a well-developed kitchen garden or small holding which you can visit.

4. Enable children to notice and support lifecycles of plants and animals through sowing seeds, hatching butterflies or chicks, or watching tadpoles turn into frogs.

5. Make stone collections including crystals and fossils. Talk about where rocks come from. How long have they been around? What was this rock like before you were born? Before your Granny was born? Where did it live? What kind of creatures were the fossils? What other creatures lived then?

6. Visit tall trees and find out how long they have been growing. Were they alive before our parents were born? Contact a local park keeper, forester or tree surgeon and ask for logs from different sized trees.

Understanding the system of culture, values and beliefs

Your individual experiences as a child, and the attitudes and experiences passed down by your parents, grandparents, teachers and carers will have shaped your own attitudes, even if you have ultimately rejected some of their beliefs and values as you have grown older. Our experiences influence the way we think and shape our attitudes towards nature, the environment and how we feel about going outside.

As teachers, it is important that we can find out and understand as much as we can about each child's experience, their family's values, beliefs and attitudes. Many Early Years' settings offer a home visit before a child starts. Whilst not all settings can resource this, it can be a very useful time to see the child in their home environment and to talk to parents in a relaxed setting. It can, of course, feel intimidating to some parents and even to some children! Whilst these home visits are usually focused on how to make the settling in process as smooth as possible for the child, such visits are also an excellent time to ask parents about their own experiences. What are their early memories? What were their likes and dislikes? What was 'home' to them? How do they feel about the great outdoors? How 'at home' do they feel in the community where they live? What are their customs? Do they have a faith? With whom do they celebrate? These questions need to be sensitively offered with no judgement and with high positive regard. You can encourage parents to share photographs if they have them.

A home visit will give you a much broader perspective on the whole child and put you in a better position to understand the environmental, social and cultural experience they already bring with them.

Finding out what makes children feel 'at home' helps you to work with parents and colleagues and, most importantly, with each child to co-create places and activities that connect them to a 'sense of place' or 'feeling at home' outdoors.

What makes each of your children feel most at home?

In practice

ALL ABOUT ME

Ask children to bring in a picture of their front door. Make a display and use it to talk about where they live and their experience of that place. Talk about addresses, and ask the children some questions about their homes:

- What is the name of the street you live on?

- What number is on the door?

- Who else lives in your house?

- What is your street like?

- What is your favourite place to play?

- Where do you like to go outside?

Ask children to bring in a picture of their favourite place to play outside. Ask them:

- What do you like about it?

- How does it make you feel?

- Where did your mum/dad/gran like to play when they were your age?

Parents' experience of nature is passed on to their children

On reflection

WHAT IS IN YOUR BACKPACK?

Your backpack contains your lifetime's experience, knowledge and skills. On a large piece of paper, create a visual representation of your personal backpack. Think about the following and write your ideas on separate pieces of paper or sticky notes:

- What were your childhood experiences of nature and how do these experiences affect the way you are now?

- Were you more of an 'indoor' or 'outdoor' child?

- Did you enjoy flowers and plants, walks in the woods or exploring rock pools on the seashore? Who taught you about nature and what did you learn?

- Did you play outside – and if so where? Were you alone or with others?

- What useful knowledge and skills have you gained from your experiences in nature that you can offer to the children in your charge?

If possible, share with a colleague or colleagues and reflect on:

- What would you like to add to the backpack over the coming year? What about the next three years? What new skills, knowledge and experience do you want to gather?

- What would you like to gift to the backpacks of the children in your care?

- Discuss how this will feed into your design and planning for working outdoors.

A sense of place

Narrative

KEN, LUCY AND ROHAN: WORKING WITH CHILDREN WITH DIFFERENT EXPERIENCES OF THE OUTDOORS

Ken's mum Sandra was brought up in Kenya. She talked about the freedom to play out with other kids in the village where she lived and how they loved to pretend to cook together. Now she lives with Ken on an estate. She has a small garden but doesn't know the neighbours. She takes Ken out to the park often, but she doesn't like the cold and doesn't feel particularly safe. She misses her extended family and has visited Kenya once with Ken in the four years since he was born.

Lucy's parents live on the 4th floor in a block of flats with no garden. Lucy is a lively three-year-old who quite literally tries to 'climb the walls'. Her speech and interaction with others is not at the expected level and she often screams loudly with frustration. Lucy's parents have lived in cities all their lives. They are surprised by how much energy Lucy has and often feel at a loss as to what to do with her. They take her to the park often where generally things are better. Another baby is due, and they don't know how they will carry on coping with Lucy without a garden.

Rohan's parents come from southern India and his first languages are Malayalam and Hindi. His parents work shifts as specialist nurses at the hospital. When Mum picks Rohan up from nursery, she often needs to catch up on sleep and Rohan is expected to play with his tablet or watch TV quietly. His parents don't have time to take him outside except occasionally at weekends when they go out to eat with friends. They have a backyard, but Rohan is not encouraged to go out there because it is dirty and small. Every summer the family spend four weeks visiting relatives in Southern India where Rohan is outside all the time.

These three children go to the same nursery. The nursery team work very differently with each child when introducing them to the nursery garden. Ken is shy and a little nervous of going outdoors at first. His key person invites Ken's mum to come and volunteer. She is in her element working with the children developing the mud kitchen and remembering the games of her own early childhood. Ken makes a friend and increasingly gains confidence and feels at home outdoors.

Lucy seems to love the freedom of the outdoors from day one, although at first she charges around at high velocity not really seeming to engage her senses and without any sense of balance, direction or regard to her own safety or that of others. The nursery staff work with Lucy's parents to get her speech and language support. They also encourage Lucy to engage her senses outdoors through play with sand and water and by creating obstacle courses which encourage staged risk awareness and the use of gross motor movement. As Lucy slows down, she starts to connect with other children too and gains more control and self-regulation in her movement.

Rohan is not easily persuaded to go outdoors to begin with, but with the encouragement of his key person he begins to enjoy sand and water experiments, transporting and construction. He makes rapid progress in speaking English, in his gross and fine motor skills and in mathematical application. Seeing his progress in language, number, movement and self-confidence, Rohan's parents talk to the nursery about what he does when he's there. Rohan's key person shares photos of his learning journeys and the progress he has made. This makes his learning outdoors visible. Following this discussion, his parents decide to clear the backyard to enable Rohan to have more play outdoors when at home.

'Nature deficit disorder' or a sense of place?

Children can more easily move, feel, notice and stretch their bodies, and learn about themselves and others when they are outdoors. Teachers and carers also benefit from time outdoors. There are always natural teaching resources present in nature – wherever you are and whatever your outdoor space looks like.

Many people have written about what makes us feel connected or disconnected to nature and the places where we grow up, live and work. Richard Louv coined the term 'nature deficit disorder' in his book *Last Child in the Woods*. He collected evidence in the USA of the trend towards less childhood time being spent outdoors and the negative impact this is having on children in many aspects of their development including their sense of connection to place. The term nature deficit disorder has been misunderstood as a medical condition – which it is not. However it has captured the imagination of the outdoor play movement and those of us who have direct experience of the decreasing opportunities for children's play in nature. We are concerned about the negative impacts of changing landscapes and lifestyles on children's development and opportunities to learn with nature.

A sense of place, of being and belonging, develops when we take time to connect with the natural world around us in a real, direct and meaningful way. We develop shared memories through shared experience – of going outdoors, of sensory experience and of significant events such as births and death, festivals and celebrations. The ways in which we teach our children will be different depending on who we are and where we live, on our faith and our culture. How we teach our children also depends on the environment and our connection to it, and whether we feel at home in this place or not.

In his book, *Earth in Mind*, David Orr compares the sense of displacement migrants experience to the feelings of psychological displacement we can suffer when we are disconnected from a sense of place and belonging. This displacement is a kind of loss of the connection between where we live and the sources of our survival and wellbeing. For example, these days many of us may only eat pre-packaged food and never experience the source of that food; our energy comes from a flick of switch rather than us having to source fuel for a fire and stoke a stove. With increasing transport options, people may travel to work, worship or school; they may spend their leisure time outside of the community in which they live. Any or all of these factors and changes in the social fabric of families, villages and cities, may mean that we also lose our sense of any connection between the place we live and a sense of belonging to that place. We lose our sense of place-based history, shared ancestry and shared memory. Changes to the physical landscape – new buildings, signs, fences, roads – environmental changes also affect our sense of belonging.

As old ways of connecting to place become impossible or irrelevant, we need to find new ways of making connections and developing our sense of belonging and connection to the landscape and people – the community and place where we live. This is an essential element of wellbeing and resilience.

We create shared memories through shared experience

A sense of place

On reflection

WHAT KIND OF PLACE DO YOU LIVE IN?

Review your neighbourhood.

- What do you like about it? What do you not like about it? Are you close to family or friends? Do you know your neighbours? What feels familiar and what feel strange? What kind of landscape and nature do you see?

- How child friendly is the neighbourhood around the setting where you work?

- What features or signs tell you about how 'child friendly' or 'play friendly' it is?

- Are some spaces fenced or walled in? How much green space is there? How accessible is it?

- What priority is given to cars?

- Are there any habitats for wildlife? Are there places that encourage children's play?

- What do the street notices, signs and pictures (if there are any) tell you?

Many people are waking up to importance of connecting to nature and preserving and understanding our inter-dependency with it – not just for our physical survival but psychologically as well. Richard Louv (*The Nature Principle*, 2011) gives us many ideas and examples of ways to wake up to the importance of giving children opportunities to connect to their ecological identity. The Children and Nature Network is just one of many growing organisations, movements and networks worldwide that recognise the importance of enabling children to understand human interdependence with the rest of nature. Organisations such as the National Trust, the Wildlife Trusts and the World Wildlife Fund have developed charters and programmes to support teachers, schools and Early Years' practitioners in this work with children. There has been a rapid growth in Forest School training and new nature nurseries where children play in nature all day.

In practice

JOURNEYS AROUND YOUR NEIGHBOURHOOD

Take children on journeys to interesting outdoor places around the community. It is better for building a sense of place if these places are not too far away and you can visit them often so that children become familiar with them, and also so that they notice differences as the seasons or weather change.

Find different ways to plot, map and tell the story of your route and adventures. There are many ways to do this. Here are two examples:

1. WAY-MARKERS

You can ask children to lay 'way-markers' at key spots (these could be stick arrows or special stones). Tell the children that you are placing the way-markers so that you can 'find your way back'. Take photos so you can make a photo book about the journey when you return to the nursery or setting.

2. JOURNEY STICKS

Take a stick and some pieces of coloured wool. Stop at various points and collect something which will remind you of that place, e.g. a leaf, a berry, a flower, a feather or a pebble. Tie the object to the stick with a different colour wool to represent the smell, sound or feeling of the place. Older children can have their own journey sticks, but you can also do one as group with different children choosing to describe the sound or feeling of a place and the object and colour of wool to represent it. When you get back to the setting, you can use the journey stick to retell the story of your trip.

Before setting off, complete a risk assessment for the activity. Teach children what is OK and what is not OK to pick up. Beware of litter (discarded needles, for example) and poisonous plants.

Older children may be able to draw a map or create a map out of sticks, stones and other materials in the garden when you get back to your setting.

A sense of place

A sense of belonging to place

> 'Our work as teachers is to give children a sense of place — to invite children to braid their identities together with the place where they live by calling their attention to the air, the sky, the cracks in the sidewalk where the earth busts out of its cement cage.'
>
> Ann Pelo

American Early Years educator Ann Pelo writes beautifully about early childhood, identity and place. She suggests that as teachers and carers we need to tune into the interests of children and the natural world, even if we live in urban spaces surrounded by tower blocks or supermarkets.

> 'Find the natural world waiting for us: cycles of light and dark, the feel and scent of the air, the particularities of the sky — these are elements of the natural world and can begin to anchor us in a place.'
>
> Ann Pelo

Encourage children to immerse themselves with nature's elements – earth, air, water, wood, stone

Throughout this book there are suggestions of how to support children to connect to place in your setting. You might do this by:

- ✿ encouraging children to immerse themselves in nature's elements and seasonal abundance
- ✿ presenting challenging questions and problems to solve about the world
- ✿ taking conscious action to nurture and protect the living world around you
- ✿ giving children their own peg and place to change their clothes or store their boots and collections
- ✿ listening to children and supporting their self-expression with a variety of creative materials
- ✿ co-creating environments enabling children to make their mark.

Children love to make their mark

A sense of place

In practice

BEING AND BELONGING

We can help children's sense of belonging by making connections between home, the setting and other places of importance (such as a place of worship and favourite places to play). We can pay attention to the journeys, which are often big transitions for children, by slowing down and taking time to notice and listen to their experiences along the way. Here are a few ideas for how:

- Build on the earlier suggestions in this chapter for home visits and for journeys around the neighbourhood.

- Talk about how children get to school and the place where they live.

- Ask parents to help children take photos on a mobile phone of their journey to or from school. They should pick a day when they are not in a hurry and can make it a slow journey. The parents might want to point things out, but should be attentive to what attracts the child's eye and, if possible, give them time to explore and decide what to photograph.

  ♦ What do they pass on the way? Consider the sights and smells.

  ♦ What are the features of the landscapes?

  ♦ What can they see out of their window (if they travel by car)?

  ♦ Does their journey pose any challenges such as crossing a road or passing deep water?

  ♦ What signs do they see and what do they mean?

  ♦ Do they pass any particular places of beauty?

  ♦ Did they notice any plants in the pavement cracks?

Make a storybook or photo sequence from the photos so that the child can retell the story at school or at home.

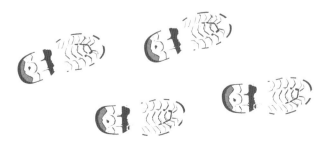

One of the aims of this book is to explore what we mean by 'a sense of place' and how we develop it. Having a sense of place is about feeling comfortable in your own skin, the developing capacity to connect with others and your environment and feeling at home. Feeling 'at home' is like a kind of radio frequency. If you are well connected, it is a feeling of clarity or being 'tuned in'; if not, it can feel distorted, out of sync and uncomfortable. As we are all essentially children of planet Earth, if this frequency is developed strongly enough within us, we can tune into it wherever our travels might take us in later life.

Further reading

To find out more about the ideas in this chapter, search online for:

- Urie Bronfenbrenner on the 'ecological model of human development'

- Richard Louv's books, *Last Child in the Woods* and *The Nature Principle*

- David Orr's book *Earth in Mind*

- Ann Pelo on 'ecological identity' or read her book *The Goodness of Rain*

- Johann Christoph Arnold on 'reclaiming childhood in a hostile world'

- The National Trust

- World Wildlife Fund

- Children and Nature Network.

A place to play – learning with the landscape

> 'The best classroom and the richest store cupboard is roofed only by the sky.'
>
> Margaret McMillan c1925

Chapter overview

Even though the lives of children have changed greatly since Margaret McMillan first opened her outdoor nurseries, the invitations and possibilities for learning with nature and being outdoors are as rich as they were when she wrote her famous quote nearly a century ago. There is practically nothing that cannot be learned outdoors, whilst there are many things that cannot easily be learned indoors. This chapter offers some thoughts and reflections about approaches to the co-creation (you and the children working together) of beautiful outdoor spaces for learning and ways of working in them.

Key ideas

- Roots of outdoor Early Years practice and concerns of our time
- Landscapes not laboratories
- The seven criteria for outdoor play
- Learning with head, heart and hands
- A word about technology
- Scale and pace
- The psychology of reading messages from our environment
- Transitions
- Biophilia and design

Roots of outdoor Early Years practice and concerns of our time

The development of early education outdoors has a long tradition with roots that extend from Johann Heinrich Pestalozzi (b.1746) to Friedrich Froebel (b.1782), Susan Sutherland Isaacs (b.1885) to Margaret MacMillan (b.1860) and then too many others to name until the present day. In the 1990s, Learning through Landscapes was established in the UK as the national school grounds charity with a mission to grow outdoor learning in every school. In the last few decades, there has been huge growth in interest in

Many formerly nature-rich landscapes have become urbanised and made inaccessible due to increased road traffic

A sense of place

Landscapes not laboratories

The children who are in our care now will be the scientists, engineers and philosophers of the future

When babies are born, they are bundles of perception. Every organ is activated with the various tasks of sustaining life, exchanging warmth, light, air, and nutrition. Every cell is responding to its' surroundings, helping the baby to make sense of the world.

The age of information has given us access to more ideas, more research and, often, to opposing views about education and how to bring up children. Technology has increased our capacity to record, measure and count things at much greater speed and to share that information widely and quickly. Measurable data has become the gold standard for benchmarking in education.

Are we in danger of turning our schools into laboratories for testing children or education theories and collecting data? Are we accumulating data to prove things we already know? Many (if not most) things about nature, including human beings, are unpredictable. Children have unmeasurable capacities to absorb, explore, follow their curiosities, create, question, reason and enjoy life.

Nature is data rich

Our education systems are in danger of dissecting learning and turning it into data. As teachers and carers, we should not lose our sense of humility and understanding that for everything we measure or think we know, there is even more that is still unexplained. When we become preoccupied with data collection, we risk losing touch with the fact that nature itself contains all the data we need in order to survive and thrive – nature is data rich. At this point in our evolution, human beings are scratching around on the surface of this data trying understanding all there is to know about our planet and our lives on it.

The children who are in our care now will be the scientists, engineers and philosophers of the future. Most well-known scientist will tell you about their childhoods playing outside and experimenting with the materials of life. We need to give our children access to the raw materials of nature so that they can develop the capacities to understand them through experience and learn how to manipulate them. We need to give them landscapes for learning – living laboratories full of adventure and unpredictability rather than pre-programmed ones with pre-determined learning outcomes.

Nature is everywhere

Nature is, of course, everywhere. We are part of nature. Babies' first encounters with nature are their own bodies and those of their mother or other primary carers. Smelling and tasting milk, listening to sounds, focusing their eyes and gradually coordinating their hands and limbs as they grasp and touch things – these are babies' first enquiries, first work and first play. Gradually their awareness of environment expands. They can focus across the room or look up at the leaves on a tree when lying outside on a blanket or in a buggy. They start to grasp objects around them and use their voices to get attention and communicate. They start to explore the tastes of different food.

forest school and outdoor kindergartens across Europe, the US, Canada and Australia. There are growing movements within the early education sector focusing on environmental sustainability, nature connection and outdoor learning. This is a time when industrialisation has eroded our natural resources and the age of technology has altered our lifestyles. There are global concerns about our climate, our diminishing biodiversity and our polluted air and seas. Many formerly nature-rich landscapes have urbanised and been made inaccessible by increased road traffic or rendered uninhabitable by industrial erosion. As teachers of young children, we are right to question what impact this is having on children's early learning experiences and the kind of education we need to offer our children for our current time.

The age of technology has brought us many gifts. The development of cameras and other technological innovations has allowed us to see under oceans and view planets in close up; technology has enabled us to get intimate insights into the lives of animals. However, these developments and the massive growth in screen-based entertainment have also brought about more sedentary lifestyles and seemingly an increasing addiction to screens. As a result, children are getting outdoors much less than in previous generations. Easier access to screen-based entertainment increases the temptation to stay indoors when added to parental fears around the 'natural' dangers of the outdoors, e.g. weather, unpredictability, animals. Global media beams news into our lives through all kinds of popular media, sharing every accident and incident, fuelling fears about what harm might come to our children and building our anxiety about what we can and should do to keep children safe.

Different kinds of play equipment and affordances of the environment

> 'An affordance is something in the environment that makes an offer to a person, or that reveals a possible function.'
>
> Tim Gill

Think about the number of different uses that children give to any particular piece of equipment or any particular space. Children's play is often more complex and extended and includes a greater range of language, learning and meaning if the play space and equipment is flexible, with variable parts, and includes lots of material that can be manipulated and changed according to the imagination.

The idea of 'affordance' is useful in the design and choice of play equipment. There are whole industries targeted at babies and young children as consumers – instant food, toiletries, clothes, car seats, carriers, buggies. We have never had more choices – there are whole superstores and websites dedicated to toys, for example. But how do we decide what kind of resources to surround a child with?

Many nurseries become filled with primary-coloured plastic and educational equipment with little sensory variety and a narrow range of affordances. Such toys have an initial attraction and draw children in with their predictability and brashness. However, the response is always the same and therefore the toy does not take the child anywhere new, e.g. 'I press that blue button so the same song/animal noise comes out'. A basket of stones, shells, scented pieces of wood combined with household objects, however, provides endless scope for touching, smelling, tasting, building, transporting or pretending. A plastic slide or a manufactured

Nature play can happen indoors too

'playhouse' will certainly attract children. But compare the experience the children get from such a slide to what they get from a landscaped or naturally-occurring hill with many different ways to climb up or down. Such a hill also offers opportunities to create a water slide in summer with a plastic sheet in hot weather, or a toboggan run if it snows. Compare the manufactured playhouse to the hidey holes and den-making possibilities of planted or naturally-occurring vegetation – clumps of bamboo, hollow tree trunks, loose logs, a small copse of trees or set of bamboo stakes and moveable poles. Nature has so many variables and is constantly changing its invitation to be used as an ever-changing den and play space – if only we could take notice of what it affords us.

In practice

NATURE INDOORS

Have a look at the resources you have indoors. What is the appeal of each piece of equipment or play material to each of the senses?

Discovery tables, displays and interactive baskets of seasonal and changing materials will be hugely interesting to the children and keep your indoor environment connected and alive.

- Fruit and vegetables – change the varieties you offer to reflect the different seasons. Use for snack time and cooking.

- Seeds from trees, e.g. conkers, acorns or dried beans – use as appropriate for sorting, counting, weighing, making patterns, artwork, sculpture and imaginative play. Sycamore seeds make great spinners!

- Dried nuts, seeds, beans and pulses – use for sprouting, cooking, eating, feeding birds or maths or art activities.

- Living creatures, e.g. tadpoles, caterpillars, worms, fish, hatching chicks to watch grow and change and to learn about nuturing.

- Rocks, minerals and shells for play, exploration and investigation. Where did they come from? How can they be used?

- Plants and flowers to smell and admire, and inspire painting, drawing and stories too.

Whatever is new and interesting to see, hear, smell and taste will keep children's curiosity alive and stimulate their learning about the natural world around them.

The seven criteria for quality outdoor play

Thinking about the design of your outdoor learning landscape is important. In a study, Susan Herrington et al. found that children had quality outdoor play experiences and enriched developmental opportunities in environments with particular features. The best environments had elements for children to manipulate and make their own, living things and sensitivity to climate. They were designed to the scale of the child and allowed the child's imagination to shape the play experience. They provided areas for children to play alone or in groups.

They identified seven criteria for quality outdoor play: character, context, connectivity, change, chance, clarity, and challenge. These are sometimes referred to as the '7Cs'.

1. Character

What kind of character does your outside area have currently? Consider what kind of 'feel' it has. Is it spacious enough or too cluttered? Is it nature friendly? Involve the children in making the space personal to your current group using plants, mosaics, signs, sculptures and weavings. Avoid creating a theme park, using plastic toys or fixtures that cannot easily be changed.

2. Context

Work with the things in your setting that you cannot change. Your landscape needs to work with nature – with the climate in your area, the type of soil, the direction of the sun, the immovable elements such as walls and trees which might become obstacles or features. Get advice on any planting you do. Notice where is shady, sunny, sheltered at different times of day and different times of year. Create warm spots and cool shady spots accordingly. Use trees, walls and fences as part of your environment – they present vertical opportunities for climbing up or along, for displaying artwork or for growing plants.

Avoid creating a theme park – use what you have in the landscape to create challenge

Walls and fences create vertical opportunities

3. Connectivity

Observe how children move and flow around the outdoor area. What gets in their way? Does the movement around the centre 'make sense' to children? Are the indoor and outdoor areas connected? Is the outdoors visible from indoors and vice versa? Are there different pathways for different kinds of mobility – crawling, running, wheeled access? Are there related resources to hand? Is there water close to the sand – and if not, is it easy to transport and make connections? Is the storage of any equipment close to where children are likely to use it, e.g. gardening tools near the vegetable patch? Put mark making stations everywhere!

Pathways with different textures also help children develop balance and core stability

4. Change

Children like a variety of environments including spaces where they can play in big groups, but also spaces to play alone if they want a change or feel more solitary. Nature also changes the landscape in different seasons and in some areas. For example, shady areas will be more useful in summer and warmer sheltered spots will be more suitable in winter. If you have 'zones' or areas for different types of activity, try to make them fluid so that they can be changed around over time. In one nursery, the children were able to change one area of their garden into a beach, then a construction zone and then a market garden over the course of one season. As the children's interest changed, so did the resources and set up – facilitated by attentive staff.

5. Chance (and the theory of loose parts)

> 'Children [should] have the opportunity to play with space-forming materials in order that they may invent, construct, evaluate, and modify their own [spaces].'
>
> Simon Nicholson

Chance is about the opportunities for children to manipulate the environment and create spontaneous or unexpected features in their learning landscape. Water and sand, a fresh pile of fallen leaves, a sudden fall of snow can all be exploited by children for this purpose. The theory of loose parts, originally developed by Simon Nicholson, has now been eagerly adopted by many designers and play-workers, introducing bricks, planks, tyres, crates, movable logs and more for children to create their own landscapes for learning. You might add a little mystery to the environment by introducing a fairy door at the bottom of a tree trunk one day or a large 'golden egg' (melon covered in gold foil) laid by a mysterious bird. What stories might this provoke? How can the mystery be resolved? Loose parts, new props and invitations will be welcomed by children and will help them develop new language skills and interaction.

6. Clarity

Don't let designers with no knowledge of child development or how your setting works tell you where to put equipment. Clear pathways for children to move in between – inside and out – and around the area are important. Whilst it is not necessary to have all children in your view at all times (hiding places are popular with children!) you also don't want unnecessary obstructions to views from one part of the site to another. Acoustics can also be important (see the section on creating soundscapes in Chapter 3).

Hiding places are fun for children – and their creatures

Add a little mystery

7. Challenge

The authors of the 7Cs research found that lack of challenge was the thing that led to the worst behaviour in children. A high-quality outdoor classroom or play area will give opportunities for challenge – where children can test their abilities and find materials they can use to extend their play and learning. This means building in a level of risk. Create climbing opportunities at different heights for different stages of development, and balancing opportunities – both fixed and wobbly. Set up hoops to throw balls into, provide a variety of loose parts for construction. Set mystery stories and challenges in motion... and when there is a real problem, ask the children to help you find the solution!

On reflection

THICKENING THE SOUP

If we closely observe the environment each day and notice what the children are drawn to, our planning will be based on the children and their interests. We can increase the possibilities for exploration and interaction, for curiosity and investigation, for inspiration and delight. We can 'thicken the soup' as Ferre Laevers calls it.

Consider your outside area from the perspective of each of the 7Cs and the characteristics and features suggested in this chapter. What are the best things about your current outdoor landscapes? What can be developed in your setting? How can you introduce new textures, colours and smells to inspire and invite sensory exploration? How might you introduce more 'loose parts' and malleable materials for maximum flexibility? How could you create new pathways and viewpoints to enable children to access new perspectives?

A sense of place

In practice

CREATE PLACES FOR ROCKS AND STONES

Gather and include all kinds of rocks, stones and pebbles of different types and colours.

These can bring so many possibilities:

- Large, rounded boulders can be used for sitting on or climbing.

- Medium-sized stones and small pebbles can be used for counting, sorting, creating patterns, painting and polishing.

- Gravel can be used to dig, heap and transport.

- Create a rock garden which could be as small as a window box or a much bigger area depending on space available. If your space is big enough, you could recreate a stone circle (a mini Stonehenge) – with boulders big enough to climb or sit on.

- Use rocks in creating small worlds with the children and develop their language through made-up rock stories.

- Children can decorate and adopt their own 'pet rocks'.

- Paint rocks gold or other colours and used as 'buried treasure' or 'dragon eggs'.

- Leave piles of large pebbles for children to use in building projects, laying trails or transporting in various ways.

- Use pebbles for counting and sorting – either plain or painted with numbers or numbers of dots (for example, painted as ladybirds).

Picking up and sorting stones is a deep and meaningful enquiry of body and mind – developing gross and fine motor movement through moving, twisting, orientating, grasping. It also develops early mathematical concepts of number, size, weight and measure.

Learning with head, heart, hands

'Head, heart, hands' is an easy way to remember that we learn by thinking, feeling and doing. Learning is not just about cognition and what we know, it is also about how we feel and what we understand. As we get older, we can learn from reading, watching videos and listening to the instruction of others. However, early learning is very much all about doing. Children absorb information about the world through their senses and learn by moving their bodies. As teachers and carers, we can ensure that children have environments that encourage them to be active, to think and reflect, to express their feelings, empathise with others, communicate their ideas and use their imagination in order to solve problems. There is more on this in Chapter 4 on sense windows.

Contemplating the fire

In practice

WORKING WITH THE ELEMENTS

One of the ways we can create landscapes for learning is by working with the elements: earth, fire, water, air, wood and metal.

EARTH

Earth is an abundant resource, but what you have at your disposal depends on where you live and on your type of soil – whether it is full of clay, chalk, or sand, whether it is dry, wet, or rich composted loam. A sandpit is essential – make it as large as you can. You will never regret the money you spend on this!

Things you can do with earth include:

• Muddy activities – there are many fantastic ideas about things to do with mud on Pinterest or other websites. There is a set of beautiful downloadable free resources on www.muddyfaces.co.uk, including the wonderful 'mud kitchen' booklet written by Jan White

• Earth for digging – at the edge of a flower border, in tyres, in containers. It is good to make it really clear to children from a very young age about where they can dig without damaging seedlings or plants that might be growing there.

• Use different kinds of earth for different things – compost for planting, chalk or charcoal for carving or drawing with.

FIRE

Not everyone is confident with fire, but if you give children early experiences of flame they will learn to respect it and understand how to keep themselves safe around it. If you do not have space for a permanent fire pit on your setting, you can:

• Use one of a range of manufactured fire bowls for small contained fires.

• Think about introducing fire to children in even more contained ways by using candles or night lights.

• Make hot chocolate in a storm kettle as a wonderful treat on a cold day outdoors.

Risk benefits are discussed elsewhere, but clearly young children need to be supervised around a naked flame.

There are ways to give children experiences of heat and energy without a naked flame too:

• Make a paper gyroscope that spins over the heat of the radiator.

• Feel the warmth of the sun – play with shadows and shade.

• Play with solar-powered lights on dark evenings and solar-powered fountains or other gadgets in the garden.

A sense of place

In practice

WATER

In the UK, we are lucky that water is pretty much a limitless resource. Wherever you are, you will likely have a natural water source – the sea, a river, lake, pond or stream. Hopefully you will have opportunities to visit these places and:

- Find frogspawn and other pond and water creatures.

- Build dams or pools.

- Throw pebbles to observe velocity and impact.

- Race pooh sticks from one side of a bridge to the other.

If you have a sloping roof in your setting (on a shed perhaps), put up guttering to collect rainwater. Play with puddles.

If at all possible, make sure you also have an outdoor tap which enables children to:

- Fill water trays for measuring volume and making experiments.

- Make mixtures and potions, cement for buildings and mud pies in the mud kitchen.

- Fill trays to freeze overnight to make ice in winter.

- Water plants.

- Mark make. Painting with water can be the most fun because you can paint everything, and it disappears as it dries. This is the science of evaporation in front of your eyes!

Reflections

AIR

Air is usually only noticed through movement – the breeze as it rustles the leaves in the trees or by sitting around a fire and noticing the direction of smoke. Children can also play with air by:

- Running or dancing with streamers or home-made 'windmills'.

- Making home-made parachutes or kites.

- Blowing the seed head off the dandelion.

- Dropping sycamore seeds off the top of a bridge.

- Making mobiles out of natural materials and things that are free and found.

- Making their own weather vane which tells them the direction of the wind.

Joy in the water

In practice

WOOD

For most of us, wood is easily found in our everyday lives, e.g. furniture, paper and the handles of tools. Other plants also provide fibrous materials which we use for building and making things – bamboo is an obvious example but there is also hemp, soya and many others.

There are more examples of how to explore wood, wool and other materials as ecological learning journeys in Chapter 8, but here are some quick wood ideas to try:

- Make stick collections for sorting, building dens, or using as tools in the mud kitchen.

- Ask your local forester or parkkeeper for small and large 'slices' of wood to use as plates, badges, signs, trays or for artwork.

- Get a soldering iron and learn how to inscribe messages on pieces of wood – the children will love to see their names carved in wood. Use wooden instruments – xylophones, bamboo bars, wooden wind-chimes.

- Have logs of all sizes in your garden for sitting, climbing and balancing.

- Ask children to make a collection of wooden things. Explore different textures of bark and smoothed wood. If you can, identify what trees they came from and have pictures of the trees themselves to refer to.

Exploring metal outdoors

Found objects can become many things

METAL

As with wood, metal can be found everywhere, but particularly in the fabric of our buildings and in our tools. Introducing children to the properties of different metals has endless scope and adds to their landscapes for learning:

- Make collections of things made of metal.

- Experiment by putting metal objects in the sun – find out which of them warms up the quickest.

- Provide real appropriately-sized metal tools with appropriate supervision. These will be much more satisfying than plastic imitation ones!

- Use metal musical instruments – chime bars, bowls and bells and wind-chimes.

- Use magnets to test the magnetic quality of different metals.

- Weigh different metals to test their density and mass.

- Make a collection of rocks which contain visible traces of metal ore.

- Recycle (safe) metal parts from clocks, and machinery for 'tinkering' or refashioning into jewellery or works of art.

- Make a board of locks, nuts and bolts that even the youngest children can safely explore.

A word about technology

Outdoor environments are most powerful for learning when they offer children multi-dimensional, sensory-rich experiences that appeal to their heads, hearts and hands. Such experiences include getting wet, getting dirty, getting lost behind tall plants, climbing trees, tasting the rain, feeling the wind, being filled with awe at the hatching of a butterfly or the rise of a big harvest moon, seeing stars through a telescope or witnessing the first fall of snow.

Children need these experiences more than ever in our digital age to balance the growth of two-dimensional visual and auditory landscapes offered through new technologies. We still have a lot to learn about how to make the best use of new technologies and screen-based learning at different ages and stages. We need more research to understand the impact of the big changes that have taken place in our lives and how they affect children's learning and development. Research will need to consider the effects of the large amount of time children are spending in front of screens but also the impact of children not doing the things they would have done prior the explosion of screen-based entertainment.

Until recently children used to experience more silence, had more time in conversation with other people, spent more time using their physical motor and creative skills, more time outdoors, and had space for boredom or daydreaming.

There are many great ways to use technology outdoors and in nature, and it has brought us amazing ways of being able to observe many formerly private and unseen wonders, such as the birth of animals in their lairs, hatching of eggs inside birds' nests and life under the deep ocean. However, this book asserts that the nature in our backyard is itself data rich – a mine of information with limitless learning potential. Children in their early years need to learn and acquire data through whole-body experiences before they can be expected to usefully process and understand it – even if they are very proficient at operating buttons and screens at a very young age!

On reflection

GETTING UNPLUGGED

Technology has brought so many benefits to our lives – creating opportunities, unimagined possibilities and new occupations.

What is your approach to using technology in the way you work with children?

How is technology impacting your life? How hooked are you? How does it feel to be 'unplugged'? In developing your mindful approach to learning outdoors, you may like to try these exercises to get you started.

Write down all the ways in which you use technology at home and at work. Try having an 'unplugged' 24 hours or weekend where you leave your phone switched off and don't deal with any technology at all. You might find this hard if you are not used to doing it. Try planning walks outside or do a stint of gardening, sports, cooking or whatever you enjoy. Take a no music, no TV, no cinema trip. Invite friends over for a meal or play an old-fashioned game of cards or charades. Read books. Write a blog about your experience and how it made you feel.

Discuss with your team how it would be to have regular days at work where everyone is 'unplugged'. What would this look like without emails, tablets, or devices of any description? This could be one day a week, fortnight or month – whatever seems achievable to you. You may have heard of Welly Wednesdays and Forest Fridays, but how about 'Tech-free Tuesdays'?

Scale and pace

> 'Some of nature's most exquisite handiwork is on a miniature scale, as anyone knows who has applied a magnifying glass to a snowflake.'
>
> Rachel Carson

When we develop our environments as places for children's play and learning, we need to consider the pace and scale at which children want to work. There needs to be space to be active and make big and fast movements. There also needs to be places where children can be more reflective and still. Sometimes you will be working in wide open spaces with sky and sun and tall trees. At other times, you will be picking up tiny shells or crawling around the woodpile with your magnifying glasses trying to find out where the snails have gone.

Children read the landscape

The psychology of reading messages from our environment

We all pick up messages from the external environment. The shape and use of public space is often a clear indicator of the values of the society or community. The design of our homes, our streets, our schools, our parks and public places all 'say' something to us and to our children about how much value we place on children's play, on the importance of cars, on the importance of trees and plants, on fresh air and daylight, on privacy or lack of it, on the safety or lack of regard or trust for children and young people, and so on. Children who are given a small area of concrete to play in with a high fence may read into this that they are not welcome or not safe, or that their needs are not highly regarded by others. Some cities have created 'home zones' within residential areas to keep car traffic to a minimum and encourage a return of street play. Playgrounds and outdoor areas vary hugely from one school or setting to another, from one town to another, and from one country to another. In England, for example, Ofsted requires secure fences, gates and locks around Early Years settings and primary schools. In Germany and Sweden, by contrast, many communities allow the general public to walk through primary school grounds, even when the children are using them for break time play or sports.

Narrative

MARY: 'WHAT DOES THAT SIGN SAY?'

From the age of about two and a half, Mary became obsessed by signage. It started when she was deeply startled by a fire alarm going off with a loud electronic voice calling out warnings and instructions. In order to reassure her, her carer took her back afterwards to show her where the voice came from and explain to her that the alarm was to help them practise in case there was a real fire. She showed her fire exit signs and tried to reassure her, but increasingly Mary asked her carers and parents 'What does that sign say?'. In most cases children asking about signs is a good indication of early literacy and curiosity about the world of text and symbols, but for Mary it seemed that all signs were warning and commands not to do things – fire hazards, deep water, one-way traffic. Signs of all kinds became dire warnings that needed to be followed and began to represent an unsafe world. Mary became increasingly nervous and fearful. To her parents and carers, it became clear how many 'don't do' and 'danger' signs were plastered around her neighbourhood – 'no litter', 'no ball play', 'no dogs', etc. As an antidote to Mary's fearful world of signs, they started to create positive signs together and looked for positive messages in text around the community.

A sense of place

Transitions

Children and babies are moved between environments and will have different experiences of indoors and outdoors and moving between them – whether walking, crawling or in a buggy or car seat. They will have different levels of familiarity with the street, home, friends' homes, supermarkets, woods, beaches and so forth. Moving from one environment to another can be difficult for some children. They need time and support to transition, whether it is settling in to a new nursery or moving between an indoor environment and an outdoor environment. As teachers, we can support transitions through the way we design and plan our environments and also in our routines and behaviour.

Children learn to read negative signs all around them outdoors – telling them what they cannot do

In practice

SIGNAGE

Try framing all your notices and signs in positive language, perhaps accompanied by a positive image or symbol – for example:

- Have you go your boots on?

- Insect hotel: be quiet here so as not startle the ladybirds

- Come outside and play

- Welcome

- Stop. Look. Listen: can you see and hear any birds?

- Please water the plants

- Has Harry been fed today? (on the guinea pig's cage)

- Walk this way

- Please hang your coat up

- Mud cooking here – dirty hands welcome!

The subtle messages children will pick up will be about how much care and attention are given to a place, how much adults value the outdoors, how much freedom and ownership they are given as children to shape it and make it their own. Work with your children to create inviting pathways, welcoming arches, child-appropriate gates and latches, windows to look through – these are all pathways of discovery; make your outside the place where you all want to be.

We can create positive signs encouraging behavior in line with our values

A sense of place

Narrative

FREDDIE: TRANSITION FROM HOME TO NURSERY

Freddie is the manager of a small nursery. She has found that if she is involved in an activity when the children arrive, they are more likely to approach her with curiosity and interest than if she is standing by the door. She finds that in her nursery the children like their parents to come in and settle them in an area before leaving. Freddie places herself facing the door but a little way away from it. Another member of the staff is always engaged in the garden, so the children can go straight out there if they choose. Freddie is usually at a table or sitting in a comfy chair with a rug at her feet. She might be engaged in shelling peas, carding wool, sorting pebbles or acorns, sewing or cleaning something.

She is always aware of each child when they come in and is ready to respond to any greeting from a child or parent. However, she is also engaged in a meaningful task, and this takes the pressure off the children. For example, Ellie might not be ready to respond to 'Hello Ellie, how are you this morning?' straight away and may need a bit of space and time to make her own kind of transition from home into nursery. When a child approaches, Freddie always offers the option of getting involved: 'Hello Ellie. I am shelling peas. Would you like to do some?'. In this example, the activity of shelling peas is a bridge to communication and settling in, and Freddie is offering her own cue or invitation – but without any pressure that the children should respond until they are ready.

In practice

MOVING BETWEEN PLACES: TRANSITIONS, FREE FLOW AND SIGNAGE

Some children are so used to being indoors that they don't find it easy to go and play outside, or they might not think of it as a good, safe or interesting place to play. Their experience of outdoor play might be limited. In order to encourage children to get outside and become familiar with the outdoors in your nursery, and to feel at home in nature, there are several tried and tested things that can help.

1. FREE FLOW

This means that children can move between the indoors and outdoors at any time without having to ask permission. Outdoor play and learning is given equal value to indoor play and learning by staff and there are opportunities to go out whatever the weather. It means that there are no obstacles which prevent children going outside and that they can independently access the clothing they need and that the doors are open (with draught/cold excluders).

2. TRANSITION ZONES

A transition zone is an area between the indoors and outdoors that feels safe and inviting. It might be a canopied area, with inviting resources just outside so they can be seen from the doorway or window. It might be the place where children change into their boots. There might be comfy seating outside, or some beautiful building blocks. It will be out of the pathway of wheeled toys and bikes which can be noisy and intimidating to children who are new to them or are particularly sensitive.

A sense of place

Biophilia and ecophobia

What is it that makes us love life and feel connected to the wider world of other people, plants, animals and the elements? 'Biophilia' is a term defined by Edward Osborne Wilson as the 'urge to affiliate with other forms of life'. He says this is a natural and innate human trait. This theory suggests that we are naturally attracted to other life and that we feel good – happier – when we are immersed in it.

On the other hand, ecophobia is the extreme fear of nature, or particular forms of life or elements. Common examples of ecophobias include thunderstorms, frogs, snakes, worms, deep water, dirt or the dark. It is difficult to know how these fears are acquired or inherited. Some of them seem to be built into our psychological make up, some are gained from negative experience, or from picking up the attitudes and responses from others. Some cultures see particular animals or mountains as sacred and others as disgusting and taboo. Some cultures value the forests as the source of all life, others are filled with stories about ghosts, ghouls, trolls or evil spirits inhabiting certain wild places.

Michael Sobel, author of *Beyond Ecophobia*, suggests that environmental education has actually increased young people's fears about 'wild nature' when it emphasises climate change, desertification, destruction of the rainforests and so on. Where it has focused on human abuse of the planet and its resources, young people just don't want to engage, as it fills them with anxiety about the future. What seems to turn people on to nature in a positive sense is hours spent in a wild or semi-wild place as a child and/or a teacher who had led them to understand, respect and love nature. There has been research into this with people who are passionate about it or who have made careers in environmental science and conservation.

On reflection

ARE YOU A MUD LOVER OR MUG HUGGER?

What particular phobias or anxieties are there within your team and how will you ensure these are not passed on to the children? Working in Early Years is an outdoor job which requires us to get down, get dirty and to enjoy it.

Using our body language, we need to show children that we enjoy being outside, appreciate what is around us and are willing to engage – with mud, worms, insects and all the science and adventure that is in nature.

Mug huggers are the adults who sometimes find their way into Early Years work, but who should maybe not be there. They come to work without appropriate outdoor clothing and they stand around freezing in winter in little huddles, clutching cups of coffee and wishing they were somewhere else. If you have mug huggers in your setting, consider how are you going to work with them so that they can become excellent teachers and learning companions with the children outdoors. How can you help them to change their relationship with nature?

In rare cases, some people working with young children seem to find it impossible to learn to enjoy being with children outdoors. If that is the case, they should maybe be encouraged to try another vocation they would enjoy more. A requirement for work with children in the Early Years should be that it is often an outdoor job!

Biophilia design principles

Stephen Kellert, a well-known architect, pioneered design principles to make buildings work with nature to enhance human wellbeing. He identified ten ways in which we connect with nature that can influence design. These principles can form a framework for reviewing your outdoor space. The list below, adapted from Kellert, has some questions you might ask yourself about how you might apply these design principles in practice.

1. **Aesthetic appreciation**: do your children get an opportunity to appreciate the beauty of nature?

2. **Mastery**: do you children get opportunities to manipulate materials and use tools to dig, channel, mould and transport?

3. **Scientific**: do your children get a chance to experience and ask questions about what they see, and make their own enquiries about birds, plants and animals and their properties?

4. **Humanistic strong emotional attachment**: do your children connect with special places and form attachments to them or to objects in them, e.g. trees or animals?

5. **Moral and ethical concern for nature**: do your children get opportunities to experience and ask questions about how we treat nature, including plants, animals and the environment?

6. **Naturalistic enjoyment**: do your children get an opportunity to simply wallow and daydream and play in nature?

7. **Negativistic fear**: do your children have the chance to express their fears and dislikes about natural elements outside, whether they have sensory aversions or other fears?

8. **Reverence for nature**: do your children have opportunities for awe and wonder to see sights in nature that make them stop and stare?

9. **Symbolic inspiration**: do your children have opportunities to tell stories about nature or use natural materials to create imaginary worlds and pictures?

10. **Utilitarian benefits**: do your children have opportunities to see how natural materials are used for human benefit, e.g. wood, wool or plants?

As teachers, we can develop our sensitivity towards the design, use and management of the outdoors to give children opportunities to connect with nature in many different ways. Throughout this book, there are practical activities and design ideas which together cover all of these aspects of nature connection. Most importantly though, the provision should not be over-planned or over-tested – it needs to work symbiotically with children and adults who play and learn together. Like nature, the design may take time to grow and develop. Everything has a season and garden design must be flexible enough to accommodate constant growth and change.

Biophillia: ways we connect with nature: Lily Horseman of kindling play

Further reading

To find out more about the ideas in this chapter, search online for:

✿ Tim Gill's book, *Rethinking Childhood*

✿ Rusty Keeler's book, *Natural Playscapes*

✿ Claire Helen Warden's book, *Nurture through Nature*

✿ Jan White's book, *Making a Mud Kitchen*

✿ Michael Sorbel's book, *Beyond Ecophobia*

✿ Simon Nicholson on 'The Theory of Loose Parts'

✿ Herrington, Lesmeister, Nicholls & Stefiuk on the '7Cs and criteria for play outdoors'

✿ Louise Chawla on 'Children's Concern for the Natural Environment'

✿ EO Wilson and Stephen Kellert on 'Biophilia and biophilic design'

✿ Randy White and Vicki L. Stoecklin on 'Nurturing Children's Biophilia'

✿ Explore the free online resource hub at www.muddyfaces.org.uk

✿ Lily Horseman's blog in Kindling Play (http://kindlingplayandtraining.co.uk/the-tinder-box/).

    A sense of place

Sense doorways – sight, sound, touch, smell and taste

'The education of the senses must be of the greatest pedagogical interest.'

Maria Montessori

Chapter overview

When we think about the senses, we usually think of five: sight, sound, touch, smell and taste. This chapter is about the importance of these five senses to child development. We call them the 'sense doorways'. In Chapters 4 and 5, we explore other senses, those we call 'sense windows' and 'sense skylights'. Together they represent a framework for thinking about children's perceptual development and learning.

Key ideas

- ✿ What are the sense doorways?
- ✿ Early sensory development
- ✿ Senses and thinking – lighting up the neural pathways
- ✿ The development of each of the senses
- ✿ Plants for all purposes and all seasons
- ✿ Sense memory
- ✿ Sensory differences

What are the sense doorways?

The five senses of sight, sound, touch, smell and taste begin developing even whilst a baby is in the womb. They are the child's 'receptors' through which children take in and receive information about the world and environment around them. Through their eyes, they learn about light, colour, shape, perspective and to recognise familiar faces. Through vision they will go on to develop appreciation of beauty, art and design. Through their ears they learn about sound, distance, orientation and to recognise voices. Through listening they will learn language, maybe many languages; they will learn to distinguish tone and maybe develop an appreciation of music. Through their hands, feet, mouths and skin they will explore the fabric of the Earth – textures, shape and consistency. Through touch they will go on to learn about the properties and textures of different materials: wood, water, rock, plastic. Through their mouths and noses, they learn about likes and dislikes, about nutrition and flavour. They will go on to use tastes and smells in order to distinguish what is good for them and what to avoid.

Through all five sense doorways children learn about the living world: about plants, about animals, about the elements of air, fire, water, earth air, and about human bodies, including their own. They will use their senses in all their work and play – whether their future is as an astronaut, artist, cleaner, gardener, engineer or accountant.

The sense doorways receive information through specialist nerve endings which transmit information to the brain which in turn sorts and organises the information and makes connections. Beyond the five sense doorways, there are other senses which we feel more internally and which are described in Chapters 4 and 5.

- *Sight*
- *Hearing*
- *Touch*
- *Taste*
- *Smell*

The sense doorways

Early sensory development

> 'People from a planet without flowers would think we must be mad with joy the whole time to have such things about us.'
>
> Iris Murdoch

A baby's senses develop in the womb. From the earliest stages of development, a baby's senses supply him or her with a constant stream of information. This information is connected and stored in the brain and helps to build the child's understanding of the world.

At around eight weeks of gestation, touch receptors start to form around the mouth and cheeks of an embryo, and taste buds develop. Smell receptors are also formed early and by the time they are born most babies can taste, smell and hear, and are very sensitive to touch. Because they have developed in the darkness of the womb, their sight will be blurry and only begin take focus over the first weeks. However, if you are lucky enough to have held a baby in the first few hours after birth, you may have experienced the 'golden hour' of wakeful attention that many babies have. During this time, they will focus intensely on the human face and even mimic responses such as sticking out their tongue and moving their head and arms.

Over the first few weeks and months, babies build their understanding of the world rapidly, using their sensory receptors as 'doorways'. As we grow through life, the things that appeal to our various senses can change – such as our tastes in food, design, music. We may also develop aversions to particular tastes, smells and colours, or sensitivities towards textures. It is worth reflecting on your own sense preferences and how these preferences or aversions influence what you offer the children.

You can also do regular 'sense audits' within your settings. By carefully observing with all your senses, you will find that you quickly become aware of what the environment offers and what needs changing. Do these observations initially when the children are not there – perhaps at the beginning and end of the day, at least once a week, focusing on different areas each time.

On reflection

AUDITING YOUR PROVISION THROUGH THE SENSES

Firstly, reflect back over your life and think about the personal sensory preferences and aversions you have developed. Then spend time in the different areas of the setting and tune into the environment with each of your sense doorways in turn. Observe with each of your senses for a few minutes at a time, before making notes in a log book. (See the next page.)

- **Sight:** What is visually appealing? What is the light like? What colours predominate? What is beautiful and what is not? How do things look from children's height? (Get down and see!)

- **Sound:** What are the acoustics like and what sounds can be heard? Does this change at different times of the day? Where are the beautiful sounds in your setting? What are the background noises and the foreground noises? Do they sound different from a child's height?

- **Touch:** What textures are there in the space for children to touch with their hands or feet? Are these soft, hard, smooth, rough? What is the floor made of? Is there a variety of natural materials such as wood and stone?

- **Smell:** What does your setting smell like? What smells nice and what smells less so?

- **Taste:** What do you grow or offer children to taste?

For each observation you make, you may have a planning action to follow up. Share your observations with colleagues or discuss them at a team meeting.

Outside sensory perspectives are changing all the time, so you need to do this exercise at different times of day, in different weathers and in all seasons.

If you can, include a few minutes for daily 'sit spot' (see Chapter 6) before you start auditing/planning. Try to keep your focus on each of your senses before rushing into thinking, planning or doing. All this sense audit data will be really useful for planning and attentive management of the environment.

Undertaking regular observations (rather than just 'check lists') also helps you become more aware of things that need looking after in the environment such as which plants need watering or that a gutter is blocked and dripping.

Indoors

Sense observation	Reflection/Action
Sight:	
The recent display is visually really attractive	Thank the person who set it up – celebrate! Reflect what can others learn from it about what makes a sensory appealing display.
Sight/Smell:	
The new plants/curtains are making the room feel fresher	Celebrate! Reflect: where else can we bring plants/freshness?
Smell:	
The book corner smells funny	Wash/replace cushion covers? Ask caretaker to shampoo carpet.
Sight/Touch:	
There are limited textures in the construction area, as most materials are plastic, e.g. blocks	Reflect with team: how are the children using this area? What can we add? What can we take away?
Sound:	
The acoustics are bad in this room	Research sound absorbent barriers/fabrics.

Example sensory audits

What's that sound?

Outdoors

Sense observation	Reflection/Action
Touch:	
This area is sheltered from the wind and is sunny today	Suggest story time happens here today.
Sight/Sound:	
There are lots of birds around at the moment	Take binoculars and bird books outside. Reflect with team on bird theme possibilities.
Sight/Sound/Smell:	
The lavender is out and buzzing with bees	Let's talk about honey – and taste it. Make lavender water.
Sight/smell:	
A rosebud is opening and the honeysuckle is smelling gorgeous	More perfume and potion making invitations.
Sight	
There is a beautiful spider web in the corner	Invitation for spider stories? Outdoor weaving project?

Listening for the sound of the sea in a shell

In practice

TRAINING YOUR SENSE DOORWAYS

We can train our senses – our eyes, ears, nose, mouth and skin – to be more aware and acute by focusing, paying attention and tuning in regularly. Children will enjoy this too.

Talk about the doorways. Stimulate and respond to children's exploration and learning through sights, sounds, smells, textures and tastes, and follow enquiries into each of the sense doorways together.

You can draw children's attention to their senses with questions (see examples below) – but be careful not to bombard them with questions which take them away from their sensory experience. Here are some examples:

- 'What can we hear?'

- 'The trikes on the tarmac are making it difficult to hear each other talk. Can we find places where we can hear each other better?'

- 'Where does that smell come from?'

- 'How can we tell if those apples/blackberries are ripe?'

Set up mini sensory scavenger hunts:

- 'Where can we find something soft/hard/rough/bumpy?'

- 'What can we see/find that is shiny like the rain?'

- 'What can we find that is circle-shaped like the sun?'

- 'How many different shades of the colour green can we find?'

- 'How many different bird voices can we hear?'

BABIES AND TODDLERS

If you care for babies or toddlers at a pre-verbal stage of language development, you can observe how they respond with each of their senses in different situations. They will enjoy imitating you if you smell a flower, they will learn to point at things that catch their eye, and of course all of the time they will be reaching, grasping, touching things (and often tasting them too!). You can comment aloud on what you observe:

- 'Mmm does that berry taste good?'

- 'Oooh that stone is cold/heavy isn't it?'

- 'You are playing with the leaves – beautiful yellow leaves.'

- 'What is that sound?'

- 'Can you hear the bird?'

- 'See this feather? It's very soft.'

- 'What can you hear in this shell when you put it to your ear? Shh, stop. Listen.'

Plants for all purposes and all seasons

Plants of all kinds are amazing gifts. They are our early relations which appeared on the planet long before animal life and have continued to evolve into so many varieties: mosses, lichens, ferns, seaweeds and fungi, reeds and grasses, herbs and flowers, bushes, shrubs and trees. All have different sensory properties; all have different gifts. Plants provide us with food, medicine, clothes, perfumes and cosmetics, paper and materials for building homes and artefacts galore. From cradle to grave, our everyday survival depends on plants and their products. If we had no other learning materials, we could provide a whole curriculum just from working with plants: science, mathematical thinking, language, history, culture, art and design, and even music.

Plants are interesting all year round. In spring, we get the shoots and sprouting leaves. In summer, we get the heady scents of flowers and the gift of grasses and grains. In autumn, we get the colour of leaves, the berries, fruit, mushroom and vegetable harvests. In winter, we get to see the shape and branches of the trees and the colour of lichens and mosses; we use wood on our fires and we search for the rarer flowers of winter and look for early shoots of spring.

Whatever kind of space you have in your setting, you will be able to grow, find and explore plants. They can be grown inside and outside – in all kinds of soil, in pots and up walls. You can bring flowers and branches indoors in vases; you can explore fruits, berries and vegetables from the local farmers' market or even from the supermarket.

The sight doorway

Eyes have been called the 'window to the soul' – they are also a doorway to the world of light and colour. Light from external sources bounces off our environment and travels through the external lens of our eye and onto the back of the eye, or retina. Our pupils, the dark centre of our eyes, help us to focus the light. After receiving focused light, the retina transforms this into an electrical impulse that travels via the optic nerve to the brain, which then makes sense of the images it receives. Receptor cells in our eyes let us see different colours. From birth, babies begin exploring the wonders in the world with their eyes, but it takes several weeks for them to focus and recognise shapes. Then they learn to reach and grab with their hands and to coordinate what they see with what they do. In your setting, children's eye height will be different from yours, so check regularly what you can see at a child's eye view during your sense audit. Nature and the outdoors provide our eyes with so many more perspectives than indoors.

A carpet of daffodils in March, bluebells in April, or snowdrops in February can all be a sight for sore eyes, as well as raising a heady scent. Do you have any flowering woods or parks near your setting that you can visit, or a space big enough to plant a carpet of bulbs to delight you and the children every year? Flowers bring colour and shape to our lives, sometimes combined with scent and taste.

Take the example of sunflowers. A simple sunflower can provide so much pleasure, so much joy, and so many learning opportunities. Sunflowers have inspired many paintings and stories including several children's books. Sunflowers can grow heads that can be larger than the children's. Sunflowers grow so fast you can measure the difference week by week. After their beautiful golden petals have fallen, you can admire the intricate pattern of the seed head and count or taste the seeds or make them into bird food.

On reflection

PERSPECTIVES OF SIGHT

Think about the close-ups of the smallest insect found under a log that sends you to get the children a magnifying class to better see its legs. Or think about the long views that 'stretch' your eyes from the top of a hill looking across land or sea, or when looking up to into the branches of a tall redwood tree, or to the stars at night. What perspectives do you offer to the eyes of the children and what new opportunities can you think of?

Do your children get close-up views that change their perspective?

Do your children get long-range views that change their perspective?

In practice

PLANTING FOR VISUAL DELIGHT

Plant your own flowers wherever you can. Nearly all flowers are beautiful, but here are some suggestions for some that will be easy to grow with children:

- Sunflowers, *Helianthus annus*: a bright, bold-looking flower that can grow up to 30cm (1ft) in height in a week! Sunflowers can be started indoors in early spring and then planted out in a border or bed in May. They may need bamboo stakes to stop them falling over in the wind.

- Pot marigold, *Calendula*: bright orange daisies that are easy to grow from seed – great to grow in old wellies (but any container must have drainage holes drilled in the bottom, so it doesn't get waterlogged inside and drown the plants).

- Mixed wild seed collections can grow a beautiful multi-coloured tapestry which changes from spring through to autumn and attracts an array of insects. Do your research and choose a good mix with lots of annuals if you want quick results.

- Swiss chard 'Bright Lights': the brightly-coloured stems and foliage of this unusual vegetable are as tasty as they are beautiful.

- Honesty, Moonwort, *Lunaria annua*: beautiful purple flower grows in semi-shade. But the beautiful pale white disc-shaped seed heads are the real treat. You can dry them and keep them for flower arrangements, collages and many other uses. The round seeds mean that it's sometimes called the 'money plant'.

- 'Chocolate Ruffles', *Heuchera*: purple leaves with chocolate-coloured undersides and pretty, pale pink flowers.

- *Buddleia* is a sweet-smelling shrub known as the 'butterfly bush'. Plant one if you have space, as you and the children will love watching the butterflies that visit.

You can use everyday objects as planters when their usual purpose is over

A sense of place

The sound doorway

That we can hear at all is a complete wonder. Sound travels through the air creating ripples or sound waves which 'land' on our eardrum, causing three tiny bone anvils to move mechanically backward and forward in response to the external sound wave. These movements then cause tiny hairs (cilia), further along, to effectively sway back and forth generating electrochemical reactions as they do, which are then carried by auditory nerves to the brain where we interpret what the sound is and what it means for us. Our ears have around 24,000 sensory cells.

Hearing plays its part in children's and babies' language development (although children without hearing develop language too). The sound landscape that children spend time in is very important. If there is a lot of background noise or music, it is hard for us to distinguish words – and for young children this is even more the case. Some children are particularly sensitive to sound and get very disturbed by sudden loud noises or if the environment soundscape is generally too loud. Calling children's attention through a mindful bell or chime, encouraging moments of silence, listening and breathing or developing sit spot practices (described in Chapter 6) can all be very helpful ways of turning down the volume and allowing our ears and nervous system to rest.

What is your soundscape?

In practice

CREATING A GARDEN SOUNDSCAPE

There are many ways to create soundscapes in your garden:

- Encourage lots of birds and insects through planting for wildlife and making bird-feeding stations.

- Hang up chimes to catch the breeze.

- Create a percussive music corner with dustbin lid drums, wind harps and cutlery chimes.

- Wheeled toys such as trikes and trucks invariably affect the soundscape – sometimes quite dramatically. If you have them in your setting, listen in often, and limit them to certain area and have 'wheel free' days so they don't dominate.

- If you have the space and ability to create continuous running water through a flow form or a solar fountain in a mini pond, this can add a beautiful dimension to your soundscape.

- When you are out and about, explore sound in places that echo, or create your own echoes through pipes and tubes or bamboo canes.

PLANTING FOR SOUND

Some trees and plants are particularly good for creating soundscapes. Pine trees sound very different from poplars or birch. Bamboo and tall grasses create their own rustle when the wind blows.

- Look out for ornamental grasses such as greater quaking grass, *Briza maxima*, an annual grass whose nodding flowers rustle in the wind; or *Pennisetum villosum*, which has fluffy white flowers and looks good all winter.

- Bamboo or bamboo-like plants are great for sound and can make lovely hiding places and dens. Be careful though because they can spread very fast and are difficult to dig up or root out if you change your mind. Plant in a contained space. Bamboo, *Phyllostachys*, is pretty and makes an orchestra of whispering and knocking sounds in the wind. Larger bamboo canes are great for making wind chimes. *Miscanthus oligostachyus*, 'Nanus Variegatus', is a good rustler.

- Love-in-a-mist, *Nigella damascena*, has bright blue flowers which form puffy seed-heads that rattle when shaken.

The touch doorway

The whole of our skin is a sense organ with millions of receptor cells in our nerve endings that respond to stimuli and send instant messages to the brain. Babies' sense of touch develops in the womb from the moment they can start making tiny movements and sense the world around them. Some areas of our skin will be particularly sensitive to touch. Nerve endings in our fingertips, for example, send information about objects we explore to our brain. Touch offers warning signals too: if you touch something that's too hot, you will immediately move your hand away because the nerve endings send information to the brain which signals danger. This happens faster than the time it takes you to think it! Through touch, children can explore the outdoors with hands and feet, and their mouths if allowed, so it is a good idea to plan your area so that they can! A newborn baby creates its first bonds through physical presence and touch, and positive touch is associated with mental health and wellbeing throughout our lives.

If you have a very nature-orientated and landscaped outdoor area, you will have a great variety of textures – stone, wood, sand, plants, mud and water. Unfortunately, many play areas are covered in 'all weather surface', which only has one texture and means you will need to work hard to introduce other stimuli to touch. Mud kitchens, sand and water are a good start. Plants can also be a great invitation to the sense doorway of touch.

Hands and texture – what can you touch in your landscape for learning?

In practice

PLANTING FOR TEXTURE

Not all plants are friendly to touch – some sting and others have thorns. Even these plants have much to teach children and if we eliminate all risks from young children's lives, how will they ever get to learn to keep themselves safe? Children also need to learn when it is OK to pick, dig up and explore and when it is not. When they are too young to understand, you will need to be vigilant about poisonous plants, potentially harmful rubbish and plants that sting or scratch. Slightly older children will learn to ask you first – can we eat this berry? Is that a stinging nettle? They will also learn that growing things die if you pull them up (to look at the roots) – and that they should only pick things that are abundant or have already fallen off the tree or plant. So, we pick up rose petals for perfume or coloured leaves for collage if they have fallen. We may pick a few daisies or dandelions or herbs for play or creative projects – but we always need to check that there are plenty left and treat the plants with respect by not over-picking. Of course, we pick plants for food, such as potatoes, salad or fruit when they are ready and ripe.

- Herbs are lovely to touch gently. Pick a leaf and rub it between your hands to smell. Rosemary and Silver sage, *Salvia argentea,* are pretty hardy and are interesting to touch.

- Different trees bring interesting explorations: Silver birch for its beautiful bark or pine cones; chestnuts or beech for their textured seed pods.

- Pussy willows are magical little buds to stroke in spring. Pick a few branches in early spring and put them in water and watch them open into catkins.

- If you have space to plant borders, include a range of textured plants such as Lamb's ears, *Stachys byzantine.* Houseleek (*Sempervivum*), also known as 'Commander Hay', is a rosette-forming succulent that produces flowers on long stems.

- If you have the chance to plant a hedge, think about a range of native hedge plants – beech, elder, hazel and dog rose rather than going for single-textured evergreen box or *leylandii.*

The smell doorway

Our sense of smell develops early on in the womb, and babies' nostrils can be seen in early scans. By ten weeks, the receptors that we will use to detect smells have already formed.

We start using our sense of smell while still in the womb. As we breathe and swallow our mother's amniotic fluid, we become familiar with its scent and begin learning about the flavours of thing she has eaten.

Inside our noses, at the top of our nasal passages we have a patch of special neurons which are unique in that they are out in the open where they can come into contact with the air. They have hair-like projections called cilia that increase their surface area. The things we can smell give off light, volatile (easy-to-evaporate) chemicals that float through the air into your nose. Things that evaporate less easily have less of an obvious smell. Odour molecules bind to the cilia to trigger the neurons and cause us to perceive a smell.

Smell is linked strongly to memory and therefore crucial for learning. Some children are very sensitive to smells. Chemical smells and perfumes can cause strong physical reactions and even emotional aversions or reactions. Some flower scents can trigger allergies such as hay fever too. (Lilies, lilac and hyacinths are particularly prone to do this.) Some natural smells are also not pleasant, e.g. rotting things, manure and stagnant water. Sometimes, opening a window and letting in fresh air can completely change the feel and energy in the room. Open your smell sense doorway as a key to some great play, learning and enquiries with children.

Scent making is early chemistry – it involves manual dexterity, balance and engages all the senses

PLANTING FOR SCINTILLATING SCENTS

One of the best things about flowers and fragrant plants is their smell.

SHRUBS

If you have space for shrubs, try jasmine, climbing rose (or any other form of sweet smelling rose), honeysuckle or Mexican orange blossom.

FLOWERS

Look for easy-to-grow plants and with strong sweet scents such as sweet peas (*Lathyrus odoratus*) and pelargoniums. Chocolate cosmos *(Cosmos atrosanguineus)* has beautiful deep red flowers that give off a chocolate/vanilla scent!

Children learn to appreciate the smell of flowers early on in their lives. They will learn that petals fall and can be gathered to make 'perfume'. If you have a cherry blossom tree, you will get a particularly prolific crop of petals! Children will make them into play confetti.

HERBS

Herbs are great for scent and flavour and often for touch too. Easy-to-grow perennials include lavender, rosemary, sage, mint, chives and curry plant. Each have very distinctive flavours when a leaf or two is rubbed between fingers.

It is good to teach young children how to name and recognise the plants that they can eat. Herbs can be used in cooking – real and play. Teach them also to know when it is OK to pick herbs (during their most abundant harvest season), how to be grateful to the plant for it offering its 'gift' to our meal, how to take care of it, and how to make sure it has enough growth left to survive.

Sharing smells in winter and summer

The taste doorway

Taste, also called gustatory perception, tells us from early childhood what is edible and what is not, what is good for our body and what can be potentially dangerous. Our tongues have between 2,000 and 8,000 taste buds on them! Taste buds form very early on, and babies can differentiate tastes based on what their mother has eaten and what passes through the amniotic fluid whilst they are in the womb. The sense of taste relies on chemical recognition of food molecules on our tongue, which generate a signal which is sent to the brain and processed there. Babies and children develop likes and dislikes for tastes early on, but these also change as they mature. Introducing children to lots of varied tastes is part of offering them a rich sensory environment for learning through this particular doorway. Taste is closely linked to smell, so flavours of food are distinguished using both these doorways.

Children eating harmful substances is often seen as a major concern when working with children outdoors – from mud or waterborne disease to the ingestion of poisonous plants. We certainly do need to do our risk assessments and take basic precautions, such as not allowing water to stagnate and checking for very toxic plants and cat or fox faeces. However, children learn early to trust their instincts – toxic substances usually taste bad! New parents often get worried about their children eating sand or mud, but manufactured cleaning products are much more toxic than most things found in nature, and a toddler would have to eat an awful lot of most kinds of mud or soil to become ill.

Tasting nature's bounty in spring, summer and winter

A sense of place

PLANTING FOR DELICIOUS FEASTS

Growing edible plants with children has so many benefits. Children learn to understand where food comes from if they see the whole process in front of their eyes and noses. They learn to respect and care for the living world through taking care of plants, including watering them when needed. There is nothing quite like the excitement of digging up a potato plant and finding the potatoes in the roots underground – like buried treasure – and then cooking and eating them with butter or a little olive oil.

Children also quickly learn to distinguish plants that are edible from those that are not. It is of course important to teach them to always have respect for the plant, not to over pick, and to check with someone (an adult) who knows – especially when it comes to berries! Many settings have fruit at snack time. This can be a great sensory and all-round learning experience if children are allowed to help with preparing and cutting the fruit. These 'helping tasks' teach so many skills for independence as well as being great opportunities for language development and conversation.

VEGETABLES – ROOT, LEAF AND STEM

If you have a space for a vegetable plot in your setting, it is most satisfying to plant quick growing annuals that can be eaten raw and taste sweet, such as lettuce and other salad leaves or carrots. Peas or runner beans – with their delicious seeds – can be made to grow up tepee poles, making shady little green tents as they grow.

HERBS

One of the great gifts of herbs is flavour – appealing to both taste and to scent. Many herbs such as basil and parsley grow quickly from seed. Perennials such as mint and chives come back each year. Bushy woody shrub herb plants such as rosemary, lavender and sage can give delight all year round.

FRUIT

Not that many settings are lucky enough to have the space to include fruit trees in their gardens – but you might find someone with an orchard nearby that you can take the children to visit. Many urban areas are developing community orchards nowadays and celebrate apple season with pressing fruit to make juice. Most setting can grow some kind of fruit such as wild strawberries in pots of hanging baskets. Hedgerows yield an autumn bounty of elderberries, rosehips (both can be made into vitamin rich jelly or cordials), or the more common blackberry. Crumble anyone?

Lesser known, perhaps, but becoming increasingly popular in restaurants, are edible flowers. Nasturtiums are a good choice because they provide such a beautiful riot of orange, yellow, gold and red flowers – however, not all children will enjoy their tangy, peppery taste. Viola flowers are pretty as well as delicious and marigold (Calendula) flower petals make great orange sprinkles. Many herbs have edible flowers too, e.g. beautiful blue borage or purple chives.

Sense doorways, memory and learning

Memory is vital for learning. Everything children take in through their sense doorways is assimilated, connected and stored in the brain. Visual images, smells, sounds and even tastes are aids to memory. Each of us may have a different preference for learning. Some will learn better through visual imagery – seeing a picture or a diagram, for example. Others will learn better by hearing things explained or through a story. A song can conjure up memories of people, places and emotions felt long ago. The sense of smell can create strong associations between particular scents and particular experiences of our past, e.g. granny's mints, newly-cut grass, school dinners, tarmac, disinfectant or a particular perfume. Some of us will learn better by handling things and feeling the shape of them through the skin of our hands.

MEMORY

Think about what evokes memory for you and what triggers memory. Is it sight, sound, touch, smell or a combination of all of these?

Think about each of the children you care for. Are you aware that they have any preferential sense or way of learning? Do they learn better by hearing instructions or a story, seeing visual clues such as written signs or gestures, or through imitating movement and actions?

Consider this question and discuss with colleagues: What memories are you hoping children will take away from their time with you? What overriding impressions do you want them to leave with?

Sensory differences

All the sense doorways are vital for learning. However, over time one or more of our senses might become impaired, or we might be born with an impairment, yet learning will still take place. We need to consider the sensory abilities of each of our children and make adaptations if needed.

Narrative

NATASHA: WORKING WITH TEMPORARY AND PERMANENT SENSORY LOSS

Natasha had worked in Early Years for many years and often supported children with hearing or visual impairments. However, one year she had an infection in her ears and perforated both her eardrums. For a few weeks, she had almost total hearing loss. She became acutely aware of how she normally used hearing not just to listen or converse but also to orientate herself in space, keep herself safe, and 'feel in touch' with the world around her. Her short-term experience of hearing loss helped her to understand more about this particular doorway and how the world might be experienced by children who are deaf. Her team explored this idea with the children. They created opportunities to walk around the setting blindfold (guided of course!) and with ear plugs in and discussed how this changed their experience – what was interesting, and what helped orientation.

Some sensory impairments such as vision and hearing impairments are usually detected early and children can get specialist support. With support, children will often quickly adapt by using their other senses differently as a way of compensating for their impairments. A hearing-impaired child might learn different ways of communicating and expressing themselves, such as sign language, whilst a visually-impaired child might learn to use their sense doorways of smell and sound more acutely to orientate themselves.

We need to take notice of atypical child responses to sense stimulus. Their responses may be caused by physiological or neurological conditions that can sometimes be complex to diagnose. However, many children present atypical responses at some point in their early years; as a teacher, we need to sensitively work out the best response and find the best means to support that child's development. You will notice that all children vary in their levels of sense perception and that some will be more or less responsive to smells, sounds, etc. Some children will respond with energetic resistance to certain tastes, textures or smells. There is increasing research about sensory processing disorders which are often, but by no means always, linked to autism. The key to understanding children's negative responses to sensation, e.g. getting sandy hands, or their apparent strong attraction to a particular sensation, e.g. the smell of rubber, is to pay attention and keep an open mind, without judgement. Discuss your observations with others and call in specialist support if you get stuck.

Further reading

To find out more about the ideas in this chapter, search online for:

❀ Child development and the senses, e.g. https://www.babycentre.co.uk

❀ Planting for senses, https://schoolgardening.rhs.org.uk.

Sense windows – survival, wellbeing, independence and meaning

> 'I go to nature to be soothed and healed, and to have my senses put in order.'
>
> John Burroughs

Chapter overview

This chapter is about the sense windows – a further set of senses which are essential to child development. They may be less obvious or well-known than the five sense doorways, but nonetheless they are essential for our healthy development. Through the sense windows, teachers can develop their awareness of children's perceptual development. They will help you to work with children to develop your outdoor environment and co-create with them the opportunities that the children need in order to take new steps in their development.

Key ideas

✿ The sense windows and child development

- Survival – temperature, hunger, pain

- Wellbeing – vitality, emotional stability, engagement and flow

- Independence – movement, balance, orientation

- Meaning – thinking, feelings and emotion, language and expression

✿ Sensory processing and integration

The sense windows – SWIM

Each sense window has smaller window 'panes' or sub-categories within it. The main sense windows can be remembered through the acronym SWIM:

✿ Survival: The first set of sense windows are the means by which we learn to protect ourselves from harm, to know when we are in danger or we are sick, and also to recognise when we are well.

✿ Wellbeing: The second set of sense windows are the internally felt senses in the body that generate a sense of wellbeing, vitality, emotional stability, engagement and flow.

✿ Independence: The third set of sense windows are the senses by which we learn to perceive and use our bodies, to leave our caregiver's side, to explore, to act on our own initiative and become independent.

✿ Meaning: The fourth set of sense windows enable us to interpret, generate and attach meaning to things and events, to develop our thinking and express what we mean and share meaning with others.

The wellbeing and meaning sense windows also give rise to our intuitive, imaginative and creative capacities.

- Survival
- Wellbeing
- Independence
- Meaning

The sense windows

The sense windows work hand in hand with the sense doorways. Babies and young children collect a vast amount of sensory information through their sensory nerve endings and their specialised neural pathways, as described in the chapter on sense doorways. This is data about their environment, their own body movement, and other beings, relationships, events and experiences. The brain collects, sorts and synthesises this information and integrates it so that the child can literally 'make sense' of their world. Of course, this happens in stages, with each new experience and environment providing new data, which in turn builds an increasingly complex picture and understanding of the world.

Babies and young children have an innate urge to engage with and explore the world with all their sensory capacities. The sense windows are powerful tools with which they overcome obstacles, become independent and learn how to keep themselves safe. The windows enable them to not only survive but also to thrive in the world, to express themselves and to develop relationships through shared meaning and understanding. Babies and young children need space and time to absorb information, and to test out their bodies and their developing ideas. They need respect, attention and positive feedback from others as they develop bodily movement and learn to express themselves through language and other forms of expression.

The sense window of survival

It is through the sense window of survival that we learn to protect ourselves from harm, to know when we are in danger or we are sick, and also to recognise when we are well. The window panes are our sense of temperature, our sense of hunger or satiety, and our sense of pain, danger and risk.

Temperature

The human body continually produces heat, and most of it escapes through the skin. Many young children do not appear to feel the cold, but they are more vulnerable to hypothermia than adults. Their metabolic rates are faster, and they have less body mass, so they heat up and cool down more quickly. Our sense of temperature is the means by which we assess temperature changes. Proteins, called ion channels, on the surfaces of nerve endings help us differentiate temperatures, from slightly warm to extremely

The sense windows are about surviving and thriving

hot. These heat-sensitive ion channels are pores in cell membranes that open, close and communicate temperature changes to the body, whether this is localised, e.g. when our finger tips touch a hot cup of tea, or more general, e.g. when we go out into cold weather. Enabling children to spend a lot of time in nature will give them lots of chances to become aware of changes in temperature. With your support, they will learn how to keep themselves comfortable and safe – independently finding the right outer clothing, drinks or shade they need.

Some experience of extremes of cold and heat will help children learn how to keep themselves safe. Many children love handling ice and snow – but they may not notice how potentially harmful this can be to their bodies, until their hands are already very painful and heading towards frostbite. When exposing children to play with ice and snow, you can help them become aware of cold and when they need to do something about it. You can say, 'Oh your teeth are chattering and your hands look a bit blue... Are you feeling cold? How can you warm yourself up?' or 'BRRRR that is a cold wind. How can we find shelter and keep ourselves warm?'. If they don't know, you can ask other children for suggestions. Hopefully they will suggest hats, gloves, to make a fire, shelter behind a wall, or they might come up with some more surprising answers! All suggestions are welcome – but clearly it is your job to make sure no-one gets frostbite, hyperthermia or seriously hurt!

Likewise, having an open fire can be a really good way of teaching children how water heats up over time, and to feel the heat radiate from the flame as the fire gets bigger. You can teach children how to move safely nearer to the fire to get warm, and how to stand back if it gets too hot. If you cook on a fire, you may need to encourage patience to allow the food to cool down so they do not burn their mouths.

Experience of ice and snow teaches many things about survival and taking care of ourselves in the elements

A sense of place

In practice

TEMPERATURE: MINDFUL ATTENTION AND BEING PREPARED

Being outside and working with the elements offers lots of opportunities to encourage children to become more aware of changes in temperature, and how to keep themselves comfortable and safe.

Before they go out, ask them to describe the weather. Encourage them to be responsible for making the decisions:

- What do we need to wear?

- What about our feet? Can we go barefoot today? Do we need wellies?

- Do we need a hat or sun cream?

Whilst outside, they may well get so involved in their play so as not to notice sensations of temperature, hunger of even pain. Your role is to notice these things through your observation and by being attuned to their needs. Encourage them to become aware of their own bodily sensations, and, if they are in discomfort, to take precautionary or remedial action. If you become aware that they are shivering in cold wind, help them to find a sheltered spot or create a wind break. If they are getting too hot running around in the sun, encourage them to notice this and to find ways of cooling themselves down, e.g. through sitting in the shade or perhaps getting themselves a drink of water. By doing this, you are also supporting them to develop their sense windows of survival and independence.

Cutting an apple reveals a star

Hunger

The sense of hunger is an internally felt response to lack of food or nutrition. Satiety is the opposite of hunger – it is the sense of feeling full. This sense is transmitted to the brain through hormones generated by chemistry in the body and sensation in the belly. A baby already has a developed sense of hunger at birth and will cry if they are hungry. As children get older, hunger can become more confusing and difficult to assess, particularly in a world where many of us have so much choice of food available to us at all times. The desire to eat can also become linked to emotional issues such as boredom or loneliness. The sense can also be confused by addiction or cravings for particular tastes and substances, such as sugar. We should offer children healthy and balanced meals, encourage them to notice when they feel full or empty, and realise when they are thirsty rather than hungry.

In practice

Mindful eating

SENSE OF HUNGER: MINDFUL EATING

Fruit snack time can be a made into a wonderful opportunity to explore fruit and to relish each mouthful by slowing everything down. As soon as they can hold a knife (nothing too sharp), children can get involved in preparing the fruit. Soft fruit like pears or bananas are the easiest to learn to prepare.

Take time to ask questions or respond to questions from the children: Where did this apple come from? How did it get here? What helped it to grow? Explore the fruit with all your senses. How does it feel? What colour is the skin and the flesh? What does it smell like? When I cut it, what do I see? How may pips? Can you see the hidden star shape made by the seeds in the core? Chew a piece slowly – where do you feel it on your tongue? What does it taste like? When I have eaten it, do I feel full?

Ask 'where do apples grow near here?' and visit an apple tree at different times of year to see the progress of the fruit. You could also buy or borrow a juicer and make your own juice in apple season.

Pain and discomfort

Research shows that babies feel pain as much as, and perhaps more than, adults. As with temperature, pain sensations are experienced through the touch doorway – the nerve endings in the skin. If we experience a sudden strong pain, like that generated by pricking your finger, neurons are activated and the muscles of your arm contract, moving your hand away from the sharp object. These signals are so quick that we usually react involuntarily even before we are consciously aware – we will have pulled our hand away before even becoming conscious of the pain.

The children in your care may have been brought up with different parental approaches to taking risks and also different ways of managing discomfort or pain. They will have different tolerance thresholds too. As teachers and carers, we should be sensitive to what young children need in terms of reassurance and comfort, from 'rubbing it better' to getting an ice-pack or plaster if needed. We can also model through our own responses that minor accidents, bumps and bruises are normal, and part of learning, and that they are not fear-filled events.

Developing a risk benefit approach

'Play is great for children's well-being and development. When planning and providing play opportunities, the goal is not to eliminate risk, but to weigh up the risks and benefits. No child will learn about risk if they are wrapped in cotton wool.'

Health and Safety Executive

Children naturally seek out risks and it is healthy that they do so. For a one year old, learning to stand upright will feel risky at first – and adults watching might hover anxiously as the baby takes their first steps. However, without being brave enough to take this risk, babies would not learn to walk. They will also pick up their cues from you, particularly whether your behaviour and responses are fearful or encouraging.

Extending our limits can sometimes be risky – but is essential for learning

On reflection

WHAT'S YOUR APPROACH TO RISK?

There is no more responsible job in the world than caring for other people's young children. Parents, quite naturally, are anxious that their child is kept safe in any childcare or educational setting, and it is vital that we are vigilant that children are not exposed to serious hazards which could endanger their life or cause serious injury.

As teachers and carers, we are used to doing risk assessments – both in our planning of activities in a formal way, and informally in our heads. Keeping children safe is central to our everyday work. However, in the general course of play – whether running, climbing or transporting materials – children will sometimes slip, trip or fall as they learn the limits and possibilities of their bodies at each new stage of development.

Playing outside presents more risks – and more learning opportunities. Some teachers and carers avoid taking children outdoors because of the perceived risks:

- more space for children to run and explore = less control

- more variables in the environment (such as weather) = less control

- unpredictability of what you might meet (such as animals and insects) = less control

- more risky elements (fire, water, plants, weather) = less control.

If we want children to grow resilient and independent, we cannot wrap them in cotton wool and never let them try new things or test their skills and ability in a situation that feels risky to them. In order to develop manual dexterity, they will benefit from using real tools, but they might also scrape or cut themselves. In the course of learning about the natural world or playing outside, they might get stung or pricked, but this gives them good information about how to avoid getting hurt in future. When solving problems through constructing with materials, ropes and pulleys, they might drop something on a toe or pinch their fingers. But such minor injuries are badges of honour – they come as the result of endeavour and they are learning experiences in themselves.

A sense of place

Children cannot learn to keep themselves safe without exposure to unpredictability and variability. As teachers and carers, we need to give over some of the control to the young children. We need to trust children's innate instincts to survive and also their capacity to learn. Being outdoors and working with nature gives all the teaching and learning opportunities needed to develop these essential skills for survival, adaptability and independence.

On reflection

RISK BENEFIT

This is a useful exercise to do with your team.

1. Individually, list the hazards you might encounter when you are working with children outdoors.

2. Look at each hazard and decide how big and severe the risk is, i.e. are children under threat of serious injury? Give each hazard a 'risk level' score from one to five with five being the extremely serious or life threatening and one being minor.

3. Give each hazard a 'likelihood' score depending on how likely it is to happen from one to five with one being very unlikely and five being very likely.

4. Check your lists with other team members. Discuss any areas where your scores vary and try to come to an agreed score.

5. As a team, or with another person, decide what you can do to modify the risk. The risks with high level scores need the most actions – or maybe you need eliminate the hazard altogether.

6. For hazards with a lower score, think: 'what are the children learning from this activity or from encountering this hazard? If we eliminated the opportunity for children to encounter this hazard, what important learning might they miss out on?'.

Talking to parents and colleagues can be helpful in developing a confident risk benefit approach. There are now many resources that explain how to undertake a risk-benefit analysis and how to develop your thinking and pedagogical approach to risk.

In practice

LEARNING ABOUT RISK AND KEEPING SAFE

There are lots of things you can do whilst outside to help children learn about risk and keeping themselves safe.

Space: Create space where children can run, balance and climb on different surfaces, e.g. wood, stone or metal.

Clothing: Teach children to look at the weather and decide what clothing is needed. Take them out in all weathers. Teach them to get themselves dressed and change their shoes when moving between indoors and outdoors.

Animals: Create opportunities for children to learn about and care for animals and insects. Teach them to understand which animals can cause harm, in what circumstances and how to behave to avoid being stung or bitten.

Plants: Introduce children to lots of different plants. Teach them which plants are edible and which are not. Let them pick blackberries and learn to watch out for thorns and stinging nettles.

Elements: Introduce children to real flames and real ice so they can experience the properties of both and keep themselves safe.

Outings: Take children on outings so they experience how to take care of themselves when crossing the road or when near deep water.

The level of supervision and control needed for all these experiences should correlate to the nature of the hazard and level of risk. Therefore, if the only risk is a scrape, bump or sting, then children will learn best through being allowed to experiment for themselves (unless, for example, they have severe allergies to bee or wasp stings, in which case an emergency plan should be in place and appropriate medication should be at hand). If the hazard might cause severe injury or death, e.g. a busy road or deep water, then supervision, and high a staff to children ratio should be in place; adult control is paramount until you are completely confident that the child can manage this hazard themselves. Balancing risk with opportunity and control with developing independence is difficult – it requires knowledge of the children and experience and sensitivity from the adult.

The sense window of wellbeing

The second sense window contains the felt senses that generate wellbeing, vitality, emotional stability, engagement and flow. They can be felt as sensations in the body but also as feelings or emotions.

Director of the Centre for Experiential Education, Professor Ferre Laevers, tells us that young children's deep-level learning takes place when their wellbeing is high and also when they are able to be fully engaged with their learning experience. He and his team have developed tools with which to assess children's level of wellbeing and engagement as a means of evaluating how effective our practice and environments are. If children are not fully engaged when we observe their play, then we need to think about how to modify or change what we are doing and/or the environment in order to benefit their wellbeing and learning.

Understanding Laevers' process-orientated approach to teaching and learning is a very good way into becoming aware of the sense windows. His tools for assessing wellbeing and engagement can be used as a way in which teachers can develop their sensitivity and practice. Wellbeing as presented here includes physical health and vitality, emotional security and the capacity for engagement and flow.

Vitality and physical health

When children are full of vitality, they have energy and their eyes sparkle, they look comfortable in their skin and they are up for anything. Children with vitality are alert and attentive, they will smile often, they may be full of questions or show other signs that they are ready to engage in play and learning.

There is an increasing amount of concern about the over-use of chemicals used in food production, building materials, cleaning products and in the air that we breathe and the impact of this on children's health and wellbeing. Some of these things are not within your control but some of them are and there are often alternatives such as organically grown food and biodegradable cleaning materials which are relatively toxin free.

After a morning playing in the fresh air, you will notice children will come in with eyes sparkling, more colour in their cheeks, sometimes breathing hard and chattering about their adventures. Enabling children to get outdoors supports their immune systems, cardiovascular systems, muscular skeletal systems and brain development. It increases the amount of oxygen that feeds the blood and brain. At a time when we are concerned about rising levels of obesity and associated health conditions, prolonged and regular play outdoors should be an entitlement for every child.

WELLBEING AND VITALITY OUTDOORS

If the air quality is good, just being outdoors will support children's wellbeing. Here are some questions which you and your team can modify and develop and add more specific actions to, according to your setting and your plans:

- There is a growing trend in 'outdoor nurseries' because of the known health benefits of fresh air activity. How can you increase the time your children spend outside?

- Babies and young children can have their sleep time outdoors, as long as they are protected from the elements with appropriate clothing, shelter and blankets. How can you give babies and toddlers options for rest outdoors?

- Children's play and wellbeing will benefit from contact with nature and with as many different natural, living and growing materials as possible. How can you enrich your natural environment?

- How can you ensure children are protected from over-exposure, e.g. too much sun?

- How can you ensure the air, food and materials around children are as toxin-free as possible?

What does vitality look like to you?

Emotional security and connection to the senses

Information from our sense doorways and our sense windows are processed in the brain not only as thoughts but also as feelings. Emotions such as love, hate, anger, trust, joy, panic, fear, and grief are experienced differently by each of us. Scientists do not all agree on what emotions are or how they should be measured or studied. Emotions are complex and have both physical and mental components. Scientists have tried to measure them in relation to individual (subjective) feelings, physiological (body) responses, and expressive behaviour. Emotions are linked to hormones, which carry messages to the brain, e.g. adrenaline, which triggers our 'fight or flight' response to stressful situations.

Babies express emotions from the day they are born. We can hear it in their different cries. As they become more self-aware, they are also able to express emotions with greater clarity.

Children with high levels of wellbeing have self-confidence and can quickly bounce back from difficulties that cause them frustration, anger or fear. They are able to be relaxed and at peace and are in touch with themselves. This enables them to adopt a receptive attitude towards the environment and any experiences that they are offered. They are able to be 'fully themselves'.

On reflection

THE SOOTHING POWER OF NATURE

There is an increasing amount of evidence that spending time in nature can lower levels of cortisol, lower blood pressure, calm us down, sooth frustrations and relieve stress. The Japanese prescribe 'forest bathing' as a treatment for some health conditions. The NHS prescribe health walks and green gyms for adults. Gardening and other outdoor activities are known to be helpful in the treatment of some mental health disorders. Teachers will know the benefit of going outside so the children 'can let off steam'. Crying babies or distressed toddlers can be soothed by taking them outside. When a child seems overwhelmed with uncomfortable feeling, a simple shift into an environment with more space and sky can help a child 'come to their senses', when accompanied by a kind and soothing carer.

In practice

OUTSIDE SPACES

Make your outside space a place of comfort and refuge with:

- green or natural shelters in which to sit or lie down and relax.

- comfortable places to sit and give hurt or emotionally over-wrought children a cuddle.

In Denmark, where the weather is cold and dark for much of the year, the Danish have developed the idea of 'Hygge' – making things cosy on cold winter days. Try:

- warm mittens and thick socks.

- a shelter where children can 'just be' in nature without getting wet and cold.

- warm rugs and blankets to wrap up in.

- warm drinks from a storm kettle.

- lanterns for when it gets dark early.

Is there room for cosiness and daydreaming in your environment?

Engagement and flow

> 'The best moments usually occur when a person's body or mind is stretched to its limits in a voluntary effort to accomplish something difficult and worthwhile. [...] For each person there are thousands of opportunities, challenges to expand ourselves.'
>
> Mihaly Csikszentmihalyi

Children who are engaged are completely absorbed in what they are doing. They will return to a particular form of play or learning repeatedly until they have mastered some skills they need, have understood a problem they want to resolve, or have finished a story or a piece of creative work they are involved in. They give the activity their full attention. They are drawing on the 'characteristics of effective learning' – they are curious, motivated, self-determining and entrepreneurial. They are not easily distracted.

Flow, as described by Csikszentmihalyi, Ferre Laevers, and others, is a state of being when we are fully engaged with deep-level learning for extended periods of time. We become absorbed, often ignoring the calls of hunger and temperature, or the demands and expectations friends, carers or teachers. In adults, flow states are often reached when we are engrossed in something we are good at – cooking, sport or playing music.

In practice

ENGAGEMENT AND FLOW OUTDOORS

Here are some examples of how you can support children's engagement and flow outdoors:

- Work with rhythm rather than routine – the seasons, the pattern of the day and each child's need for activity, rest and food.

- Allow children time to engage fully in their play and learning – if possible, don't clear things away before they are finished with them.

- Allow children to move freely between indoors and outdoors for as much of the session as possible.

- When you observe children deeply in the flow of play and learning, try not to interrupt it with unnecessary questions, interventions or routines.

Children need time for engagement, free from unnecessary interruption, to be able to experience flow states – the joy of being fully immersed in something. This is when they are mastering new skills and learning to excel at things. This starts with babies and toddlers who rehearse movements or tasks again and again when learning to roll or crawl, for example. In older children, it might be when they are learning to skip, whistle or mix mud to just the right consistency for the building project they have in mind. There should be space outdoors to engage in repeated and extended tasks, including allowing children to return to what they were doing the day before, and perhaps even seeing how things have changed overnight. This enables children to develop persistence, determination and satisfaction in their work.

On reflection

ENGAGEMENT, FLOW AND TECHNOLOGY

Technology is embedded into every part of our existence these days. Elsewhere in the book I have discussed the gifts and the risks that technological developments have brought to young children. However, it well worth exploring this theme with your colleagues in relation to flow.

Babies and young children seem to be naturally and instinctively drawn to the flicker of screens and to the interaction afforded by the buttons of a keyboard. Screens engage the eyes and the brain without the need to use other parts of the body; when sitting in front of screens, the body becomes sedentary and still. Even where there is interactivity, it often involves repetitive movements of the hand rather than offering any sensory variability or learning beyond a certain point.

Parents in your setting might have very strong views about the importance of early exposure to learning through technology or they may be against it.

With your team, discuss each of these questions for each age group of children in your care:

- What are the benefits of enabling young children to engage with technology? What do they learn from these activities?

- What, if anything, are they not learning during the time spent in front of a screen. Are they missing out? Does it matter?

- What is your policy about including technology in your offer and how will you explain your approach to parents?

The sense window of independence

The third sense window relates to all the others. It is the job of teachers to help children become independent and able to survive and thrive in the world. They need to learn many things – in fact all the things contained in each of the sense windows – in order to do that. However, here we focus on physical independence in terms of balance, movement and orientation, and what babies and young children need to learn about their bodies to begin to leave their caregiver's side, to explore, to act on their own initiative and become physically independent.

Movement and balance and spatial awareness

> 'The question is not how we can "teach" an infant to move well and correctly, using cleverly though up, artificially constructed, complicated measures, using exercises and gymnastics. It is simply a matter of offering an infant the opportunity – or, more precisely, not to deprive him of this opportunity – to move according to his inherent ability.'
>
> Dr Emmi Pikler

As well as receiving information through the sense doorways, a baby's or toddler's time will be taken up with getting to know how their own body works, learning how to coordinate movements of head, limbs and trunk and how to make intentional movements towards objects. There are several systems in the body that help us to ultimately learn to stand upright and travel with free hands. This huge development task takes up a lot of energy in the first year or two of life. Standing upright and building core strength is essential for young children before they can grasp things and use tools or a pencil. For mark making, they need to coordinate their hands with their vision – requiring focused attention and stability.

The vestibular system regulates our balance and is very sensitive to subtle changes in position or movement. It uses the semi-circular canals in the inner ear to receive information about movement, change of direction, change of head position, change in gravitational pull, and any changes in direction or speed.

The proprioceptive system is located in the joints, muscles, and tendons. It uses tiny receptors located in the body to receive information from the contraction and stretching of muscles, and from the bending, straightening, pulling, and compression of both the joints and the nervous system, which sends this information to the brain. This enables us to interpret where our body parts are in relation to each other.

The development of spatial awareness and orientation enables us to learn about how our bodies are placed in relation to other objects and the environment. This is essential in order for a child to develop a sense of direction and learn how to travel without bumping into other objects. This is sometimes called kinaesthetic awareness. As children develop their awareness of objects in relation to themselves and other objects, they learn about speed and distance. Their movements become more controlled and they become more aware of their personal space. Spatial awareness is required to understand many mathematical concepts such as volume, shape and area.

Being outside offers so much more scope for developing movement, balance and orientation. It is important to review what kind of environment you are offering to young children. If they always walk on pavements or are transported too much in buggies and car seats, they do not get the opportunities to flex and extend their muscles and respond to variation – all of which they need to gain control of their bodies, free their hands and find their way around.

Surfaces designed purely with 'safety' in mind can often be uniform and mono-textured, limiting the use of muscles to certain muscle groups, and not giving sufficient stimulation to develop core stability and good posture. Ultimately, if children do not get good and varied opportunities, it puts them at risk. If they do not have the opportunities in less predictable environments, such as the rough surface of a forest path or a cobbled pavement, they may not develop balance and core strength. They risk being more prone to clumsiness and bad posture and may lack the stamina and strength they need.

Going barefoot helps children learn balance and develop flexibility. It helps them to feel and connect with nature

On reflection

TOUCHING THE EARTH

Why is it that we have become uncomfortable about taking off our shoes? In many countries, children walk barefoot by virtue of custom or poverty. If you have the chance to watch them, their posture is often more upright, and their movement are often more coordinated, agile and graceful than those of their shoe-wearing counterparts in the UK.

If children do not experience different textures from babyhood, they can find it challenging to process these sensations later on, and they may be reluctant to walk on sand or grass, for example.

Review your practice about shoe wearing in your setting. What is your current practice? What are the reasons for it? Are there ways in which you can increase the amount of time children can walk barefoot? Would any of the staff consider setting an example and spend time being barefoot when working with children outdoors? If you haven't done it before you might find you really enjoy it!

Getting a stone out of a welly – managing your outdoor clothes and footwear develops independence

In practice

DEVELOPING BALANCE AND ORIENTATION OUTDOORS

Here are some things you can do to develop balance and orientation in young children.

Touching the earth

- Allow babies to sit, roll and crawl freely on different textured ground, including grass.

- Allow toddlers and children to go barefoot whenever it is warm enough, e.g. on grass, sand, rocks or any surface free from hazardous or sharp objects.

- Take children to places where surfaces are uneven, such as beaches, woodlands, earthy tracks and areas with muddy puddles.

Landscape features you could offer

- Different textures to walk on, e.g. bark, sand, gravel, moulded concrete, cobbles

- Steps and slopes

- Balancing logs of different heights, sleepers or log rolls

- Pathways which wind around other features, e.g. clumps of vegetation or planted tyres

- Places to hide – and be found

- Tunnels and bridges.

Activities (age dependent)

- Games such as hide and seek, follow my leader, musical statues

- Treasure hunts with clues

- Dance and movement of all kinds

- Observing animal and insect tracks and watching the way they move

- Learning to use a compass to find directions

- Building a sundial and tracking the movement of sun and shadows

- Watching the movement and changes in the moon and star constellations.

A sense of place

The sense window of meaning

Humans collect information about themselves, others and their surroundings and the world through their sense doorways. The information passes through our nervous system, is synthesised and ordered in various parts of our brains and stored as thoughts, concepts and feelings in mind and body memory. Babies and young children also absorb ideas, feelings, customs and culture from the responses they receive from other people, the environment and events. We give meaning to what we perceive through our thoughts, our felt senses and bodily responses. We give expression to these thoughts and feelings through language and other expressive actions.

Meaning: concepts, ideas and problem solving

Concepts are our ideas – our 'mental formations' about the world – and they are refined through the sense windows as we become more aware of ourselves as separate from others and our environment. Our thinking helps us 'make sense' of the world by creating order and structure. We share our thoughts through language and expression. The concept of self or 'I', which usually develops at around 18 months, is of fundamental importance and seems to be a distinctly human concept. The environment and culture in which we are born also shapes our concept of self – our ideas about identity and all things related to it, including gender, race and sexual orientation.

Our sense window of meaning is involved in problem solving, developing ideas and making connections between ideas. Working outside and with nature helps children develop a broad set of concepts about life, how the world works, and early scientific thinking and problem solving. Nature offers us real experiences which provoke questions, investigations, ideas to be tested, and problems to be solved.

Solving problems in nature

THINKING, PROBLEM SOLVING AND MAKING MEANING

Ask children to help you solve everyday problems that present themselves outdoors:

- How are we going to transport this pile of earth from here to there?

- How can we set up a watering system for plants?

- How can we stop the squirrels from eating the bird food?

Children will come up with their own questions, so be prepared with answers or to help children find answers themselves. Here are some typical questions:

- Why are the leaves turning yellow? (It was autumn.)

- Where does the water go when it soaks into the ground? (We had emptied the water tray into the flower bed.)

- What does dead mean? (We found a dead beetle.)

- Where do butterflies live? (We saw our first butterfly in spring.)

- How can we get across this stream? (We went to the woods.)

You can also provoke questions and thinking by setting up ecological or geological investigations, e.g. How can we find out where snails go when it gets dry outside? How can we find out how many kinds of birds live in our area? How can we find out what woodlice like to eat or how long it takes for tadpole to turn into a frog?

Meaning through felt sense, body memory and metaphor

Once received by the brain, sensory information is sent to different areas of the brain for processing. Broadly put, the somatosensory cortex is responsible for physical sensation, the frontal cortex is in charge of thinking and the limbic system is linked to emotion. Our physical sensory experience is processed so the brain can learn about actions and consequences and about whether an experience or sensation feels pleasant or not.

Our direct sensory experiences, such as sounds or smells, can be stored in our conscious or unconscious memory. We also learn consequences: if I touch something hot, I get burned! Our experiences are also interpreted through the lens of our social and cultural values – the ways in which our family and caregivers respond to experiences that teach us whether something is good, OK, bad or shameful. Some experiences seem to go straight into our subconscious memory and can develop deep associations with particular centres or parts of our body – as 'felt sense' or 'embodied sense'. For example, we might experience excitement and enjoyment as a tickling feeling in our stomach, or a sense

of dread might be experienced as heaviness in the chest or the feeling of a 'dark cloud' across our mind. These felt senses form our intuition and affect our response to people and situations in the present and in future. Body sensations can trigger memories in different parts of our anatomy and energetic system. Perhaps this explains why language is full of body part and sense doorway metaphors, such as 'I have a gut feeling', 'I felt heartbroken', 'She was a sight for sore eyes', 'I smelled a rat', 'I was down on my knees' or 'I blushed with shame'.

The links between sensation and emotion and how they are stored in the memory of body and mind is complex and is increasingly used in therapeutic approaches to emotional disorders such as post-traumatic stress. Therapists, including some play therapists or trauma specialists who work with somatic movement, might ask children to describe or express their feelings as movement or describe them as sensations felt in parts of their body. This can help children give expression to things which have been 'locked inside' and help them move through them. It can help them understand better the meaning or cause of particular behaviours.

As Early Years' teachers or carers, we can become more aware of how and where children store difficult but also positive memories.

'We have no conscious recollection of our early childhood experiences, but they remain with us, embodied in our 'flesh and blood'. They influence how comfortable we feel in our own skin, how we behave in relationships and how susceptible we are to psychological problems. The first few years of life are thus vitally important to our mental and emotional development.'

Ines Possemeyer

On reflection

NATURE METAPHORS AND FEELINGS

Nature can provide us with many other forms of language and metaphors that help us to notice and describe our embodied experiences and feelings, and to understand and work with them. For example, we might say 'He was flighty like a butterfly and stubborn as a mule', 'The sky is your limit – so reach high', 'I got into deep water and nearly went under', or 'My mind is like a fog so I can't think straight'. How many nature metaphors can you think up or invent with your team or with your children?

Eddy's tiger walk helps him talk about his journey outside

A sense of place

In practice

SUPPORTING CHILDREN TO EMBODY AND EXPRESS FEELINGS OUTDOORS

There are many ways to do this. Here are two suggestions:

1. Encourage children to identify and talk about their feelings outdoors. Take a favourite puppet or teddy outdoors and ask the children these questions to prompt discussion:

- Where would Teddy feel happy out here?

- Is there anything that would scare him or make him unhappy?

- What would he find exciting?

2. If the children are old enough, you could make 'feature creatures' out of clay. They don't have to represent real animals – just a creature that children personalise. You could use pebbles and sticks to create eyes and a mouth. Take the creatures outside and ask 'Where would your creature feel happy out here? Do they like sunlight or shade? Grass or stone? What do they need to make themselves feel safe?'.

Clay feature creatures allow children to imagine, tell stories, share feelings

Sense of expression

How children acquire language is the topic of intense debate. For the purposes of this book and our framework of senses, we take the sense of language to be an innate disposition and structure that helps us to share meaning with others. Language itself is the end product of a complex process in which the speaker's inner world is shaped, transformed and uttered as spoken sentences. As the listener, we are barely aware of the surface sounds and structure of the speech itself, but we listen to become aware of the inner thoughts, ideas and feelings being conveyed by the speaker. Language has both a surface structure and a deep structure that helps us share meaning with others. The study of linguistics and the current teaching of phonics puts a great deal of emphasis on decoding this surface structure of language. Language as a means of making and sharing meaning, on the other hand, seems to be more of an innate capacity or drive in all babies and young children. Humans have evolved a sophisticated set of bodily tools – the mouth, larynx, lungs and the linguistic neural pathways in the brain – to harness this deep innate structure and share complex concepts and ideas, stories and dreams.

Narrative

ZOE: CONVEYING MEANING THROUGH WORDS

Zoe, aged 14 months, walked around for days waving her hand in the air saying 'giggle giggle' whilst desperately looking at her caregiver, who knew that she was trying to convey meaning but could not understand the words. On about the third day, Zoe's caregiver suddenly realised that Zoe asking her to sing 'twinkle twinkle (little star)'. This was her favourite song and she always listened with rapt attention. The next time Zoe waved and said, 'giggle giggle', her caregiver immediately said, 'You want me to sing Twinkle Twinkle?' and sang the song. Zoe's face lit up with huge joy and relief – she had been able to form words to convey meaning and this meaning had finally been understood and affirmed. This was a big milestone in her development of language and self-expression. She now had confidence to try other words and sounds.

On reflection

NATURE'S LANGUAGES

Nature speaks to us in many languages too: the tinkle of the stream, the whisper or howl of the wind, and the lapping or crashing of the sea. The communication of animals has been studied by humans for thousands of years. Each species has its own form of expression and communication: a mating call from a bird is different from its alarm call; bees communicate to the hive about where to find good honey through an elaborate 'wiggle dance'; and, although we do not hear them, trees communicate to other trees and plants through a complex system of roots and underground fungal spores.

People living more closely in touch with nature, such as tribal groups in the Amazon or nomads on the plains of Mongolia, will know how to read the signs of the weather and the seasons because their safety and survival can depend on this knowledge. This applies to gardeners and mountain climbers too. Indeed, anyone who spends long periods immersed with nature will learn to read the various languages of nature.

The languages of nature have inspired poetry, prose, music, art, sculpture and dance. Both observing nature and listening to it have informed and enlightened philosophers and scientists, storytellers, poets and spiritual leaders of all faiths and beliefs.

How you support children to become attuned to and inspired by the languages of nature? How do you create outdoor places in which nature can 'speak' to the children in your care?

100 languages of children – there are so many ways children can express themselves outdoors

A sense of place

Expression – 100 languages

While humans have a uniquely sophisticated verbal and written system of language and communication, ordinary conversation is not always adequate to convey what we mean. As a result, we have developed many other forms to communicate our thoughts and emotions, such as poetry, music and art.

Loris Malaguzzi (1920-1994) was the pedagogical leader of the Reggio Emilia Early Years philosophy. Malaguzzi wrote the poem 'The One Hundred Languages of Children' which has been an inspiration to many teachers and carers of young children. The Reggio Emilia approach, which takes children's potential for creative expression as central to its early learning pedagogy, has influenced teachers and carers across the world. Malaguzzi's poem encapsulates the multitude of ways in which children express their ideas, thoughts and feelings beyond the structure of written or spoken words.

In practice

ENCOURAGING THE HUNDRED LANGUAGES OF CHILDREN OUTDOORS

Just as there are more than a hundred languages, there are also literally thousands of ways you can encourage children to express themselves outdoors. Here are just a few ideas to get you started. There are suggestions for further reading at the end of the chapter too.

- **Mark making:** Have materials for mark making, drawing and painting everywhere! Brushes with water for walls and trees, sticks to draw in the sand, chalk to draw on pavements are all great ideas. Make charcoal in a biscuit tin in the fire.

- **Sculpting:** Use mud and clay to make shapes and pies.

- **Land art:** Use materials that are abundant in any season to create land pictures.

- **Crafting:** Use found materials for weaving and mobiles.

- **Dreaming:** Allow children space for daydreaming, humming, singing, sitting and, of course, sleeping if they need it!

- **Music:** Use nature's materials to make musical instruments. Use nature sounds, e.g. the wind and the birds, to inspire your songs.

- **Dance:** Use movement in nature to inspire creative movement with children. Stand tall as a tree, crawl like a caterpillar, fly like bird and stalk like a cat.

Sensory processing and integration

The sense windows work closely with the sense doorways. The sense of movement is primarily focused on balance and proprioception, but these work together with the sense doorways in so many ways. For example, when your senses of movement and balance have developed, you can catch a ball by reaching for it whilst both you and the ball are in motion. You use sight to see the type of movement taking place and judge the speed, range and direction of the ball. The senses involved in spatial awareness, direction and orientation work with hearing as well as sight. We use sound to judge the place of things outside of our range of sight, e.g. to predict the speed of an approaching car.

When the sense windows are out of balance it can lead to compulsive or addictive behaviours, such as repetitive movements. Sometimes these are phases of development, schemas or experiences that young children need in order to make sense of the world or to exert their own control on it. However, repetitive or compulsive behaviours might also lead to harm, e.g. repetitive movement which involves head-banging.

It is only with experience and sensitivity that teachers can learn the difference and decide what, if any, intervention is needed. If you are concerned about a child's sensory behaviours, it is always useful to look at the whole child and how they are engaging over the course of a day or a week. If you continue to be concerned, you should seek support from a psychologist or other specialist adviser.

Children with sensory impairments in one of their sensory systems will often compensate by developing acuity and skill in another. The integration and processing of the complex sensory systems can be very challenging for some babies and young children. As teachers and carers, when you notice that a child has atypical sensory development, you will need to discuss this with their parents or caregivers. You may need to call on specialist advice and support for the child to build one sensory system or to compensate for any impairment. Supporting one sensory system can support the whole child to thrive.

Further reading

To find out more about the ideas in this chapter, search online for:

Survival

- ❀ Katherine Solly on 'risk and outdoor play'
- ❀ Tim Gill on 'no fear'
- ❀ Wellbeing
- ❀ Ferre Laevers on 'wellbeing and engagement'
- ❀ Mihaly Csikszentmihalyi on 'flow' or read his book, *Flow*

Independence

- ❀ Jan White on 'movement outdoors'
- ❀ 'Pikler-Lóczy' and 'movement and orientation'
- ❀ Angela J Hanscomb's book, *Balanced and Barefoot*
- ❀ Sally Goddard Blythe's book, *The Well Balanced Child*

Meaning

- ❀ Juliet Robertson on 'Creative and Critical Thinking Outdoors'
- ❀ Suzanne Simard on 'how trees talk to each other'
- ❀ Loris Malaguzzi's poem, *The One Hundred Languages of Children*
- ❀ Elizabeth Jarman's book, *A Place to Talk Outside*

Sensory processing and integration

- ❀ Eugene Gendlin on 'felt senses and body memory'
- ❀ Sarah Lloyd's book, *Improving Sensory Processing in Traumatized Children*.

Sense skylights – values for a living world

> 'Earth Care, People Care, Fair Share.'
>
> David Holmgren

Chapter overview

Previous chapters have offered insights into perceptual development through the sense doorways and the sense windows. Both of these are very much connected to children's physical, emotional and cognitive development. The sense skylights are different. They are essentially the beliefs, dispositions and values that illuminate what we do and why we do it. They develop in us as subtle and implicit 'felt senses' about what is right or wrong, good or bad, healthy or unhealthy. The number of sense skylights is actually limitless. Every teacher will have their own values and will be able to choose the sense skylights that are important to them. This chapter explores the skylights and how they relate to values-based teaching, mindfulness, learning outdoors and connection to nature. It provides some useful starting points for you to think about how you make your values explicit in your work, and how you share them if you work in a team.

Key ideas

✿ Sense skylights are values

✿ Beyond British values – values for the living world

✿ Approaches to teaching and learning values outdoors

✿ Kindness, freedom, fairness, equality

✿ Purpose, connection

✿ Ecological identity and Earth-mindedness

The sense skylights are values

The sense skylights help teachers and carers understand how children's beliefs and values translate into behaviour towards themselves, others and the environment. The light shining through our sense skylights will change and shift in colour as we grow in life experience. Our values change as we are influenced by other people, experiences and environments. However, what children encounter in their early years will shape the framework of their values for life.

- *Kindness*
- *Equality*
- *Fairness*
- *Freedom*

The sense skylights

As teachers and carers, the sense skylights help you to consider your own beliefs and values, and help you look at how you pass them on to children through what you say and how you behave when you are with children. Values act like a kind of guiding light or a compass by which we decide right from wrong and distinguish beneficial actions from harmful ones. Children develop dispositions and moral or spiritual beliefs based on what they learn from their families, other children, and other adults. They will also learn from their surroundings and the environment. The values that we consider important vary from one family, culture or community to another across the world. By using nature as our resource for teaching and learning, we can connect to values that are inclusive of all people, as well as values that honour the wider living world on which we all depend. Values are sense skylights because they illuminate what we do and why we do things – both as individuals and in the collective such as in our families, within a group of friends, or at a place of work.

Values are held individually (within each child and member of staff) and collectively (in a family or an Early Years setting). They are often unspoken and 'internal' but they affect the way we behave towards ourselves, others and the environment.

Values are not visible until they are expressed and shared. On an individual level, our values arise as thoughts and 'felt senses', connected to our emotions and the deeper structures of language and meaning. Often, we don't share our values verbally, but we might express them through our behaviour, e.g. through acts of kindness or sharing things with others. When we do talk about values, we often use language connected to our bodies, our feelings and nature, e.g. 'They were very kind-hearted folk', 'I feel it in my bones that something is not right', 'The injustice of it weighed heavily on him'.

Collective values are made explicit when a group of people agree on 'values statements', e.g. the 'British values' which are currently part of the curriculum in England, or the United Nations Conventions of the Rights of the Child. In the workplace or in our family, we behave in particular ways which are seen by others, but why we are doing this is not always clear to people outside the group. It can be difficult for a newcomer to 'learn the rules' if they don't understand the underpinning values of 'where we are coming from'. So, if you are working together, it is useful to reflect on and review your group values out loud – particularly when new people join.

On reflection

WHAT ARE YOUR VALUES – YOUR SENSE SKYLIGHTS?

Over the last century there has been growing social and political value placed on economic growth and consumerism, often at the expense the natural resources of the planet such as oceans, trees, animals and at the expense of other human lives. Working with children outdoors can bring some of these conflicting values to the fore.

Take some time to consider which values are most important to you, and which values are most clearly part of the way you work as a team. Ask every member of your team to write a list of their core values – those that are important to them. Use the questions here, and other open questions of your choosing, to prompt a discussion about values with those that you work with.

• Do we have a strong ethos of kindness and cooperation?

• How do we respond to differences in opinion about what freedom or equality mean?

If you teach in the UK, British values will be part of the statutory curriculum. What do you think of these values? How do you make them real and bring them alive in your work with children and with your team if you have one?

What difference do your own values and the values of the team make to the expectations of how children behave towards each other and the environment?

Do you already have a values statement in your brochure or somewhere parents can see it? How does this get reviewed and renewed?

A sense of place

Beyond 'British values' – values for the living world outdoors

In England, since 2014, the statutory Early Years Foundation stage includes new responsibilities for schools and registered Early Years settings to teach British values, according to the Prevent duty and in light of national concerns about radicalisation and terrorism. British values are named as:

✿ Democracy

✿ The rule of law

✿ Individual liberty

✿ Mutual respect

✿ Tolerance of different faiths and beliefs.

When the new regulations were first introduced, there was much confusion as to what these values really meant in practice, and how to make these values 'visible' within Early Years nurseries, playgroups and other registered settings. Gradually, Early Years practitioners began to look at how these five values related to their already deeply-held values and practice. Many places found that the values were already embedded in what they do, and that the discussions around values were very useful in making visible what they believe and what they communicate to children.

For practitioners who are passionate about values that encompass the wider living world, and who understand that we are all connected and interdependent with nature, talking about values is a chance to embrace this too. Working outdoors provides ample opportunities to learn about nature and extend our values to the wider living world.

Beyond 'British Values' to values for the Earth

Mutual respect
- Care for nature's living things, including care for each other
- Grow and share food, water plants, care for animals
- Time WOW moments of awe and wonder for the miracles of life
- Respect for the power of nature including its life-limiting potential
- The need to take care of life (our own and others)

Tolerance
- Notice and celebrate children's and their families' different responses to nature
- Listen to and don't judge children's beliefs and responses to big questions of life
- Use nature as a teacher

Rule of law
- Explore laws of nature
- Rules of keeping ourselves safe
- Experience fire, water, plants and animals
- Learn appropriate rules for responding to fire, water, plants and animals

Democracy
- Use nature and other children as your teachers
- Use companioniable critical enquiry to learn about what is going on in nature
- Share home-grown food crops fairly
- Talk about rights and responsibilities of people and also of insects and animals

Individual liberty
- Develop independence through physical challenges outdoors
- Learn self-care, e.g. putting on outdoor clothes
- Experience freedom of movement outdoors, e.g. running and climbing
- Talk about the right of wild birds, animals and flowers to be free of captivity

A sense of place

Pedagogical approaches to teaching and learning values outdoors

As teachers and carers of young children, you will find some pedagogical approaches that work better than others for teaching and sharing values. Just 'telling' cannot work, as values develop slowly through experience and change as our thinking and beliefs are shaped over time by the places we visit, the things we read, the people we meet and the conversations we have.

You can use sound pedagogical approaches such as asking open questions, coaching and critical inquiry to prompt and stimulate children's sense skylights.

What do your friends here think about that?

In practice

PEDAGOGICAL APPROACHES TO TEACHING AND LEARNING NATURE VALUES

You can:

- Allow children time to work things out through their role play and give them lots of time to explore and reflect.

- Model behaviour and walk your talk – demonstrate your values by your actions – young children are acutely observant!

- Comment and ask questions in a non-judgemental way about behaviour you observe, e.g. 'That was a kind thing to do Josh' or 'What would be the fairest thing to do now?'.

- Allow space for feelings that arise spontaneously in nature, particularly around sometimes difficult issues of impermanence, suffering or change.

Very young children are deeply interested in these matters. Consider how often a three-year-old asks 'why'. Working outdoors, we can look for those 'teachable moments' when a child asks those 'awkward' questions, e.g. 'Why can't we pick the flowers?', 'Why do some people pick flowers and put them in shops?', 'How did the bird die?', 'Did God make centipedes?' or 'Why do some people eat animals?'.

We can find out what thinking lies behind these questions by asking questions back: 'That is an interesting question, what do you think about that?', 'What do you know about that already?' or 'What a great question – how can we find out the answer?'. Allow time and opportunities to share different views and to test out ideas and answers!

A sense of place

Kindness and compassion

When we talk about values, we often talk about 'doing good'. But putting values into practice does not mean taking ourselves too seriously. Being kind can be fun – mischievous even! Kindness is the opposite of doing harm. It is related to empathy and compassion, but there are differences. Empathy is being able to take the perspective of, and feel the emotions of, another person – it's being able 'to walk in their shoes'. Compassion is similar to empathy, but includes sensitivity, particular to the suffering of others, and the desire to help. As teachers and carers of babies and young children, we all want to encourage kind behaviour.

On reflection

THE MEANING AND PRACTICE OF KINDNESS

Encouraging kind behaviour can take many forms. It is worth thinking about what you mean by kindness personally and professionally and what it looks like in your work with children. What do others in your team think? How can care of plants and animals teach kindness?

When we spend time outdoors, children can learn to extend kindness beyond their family and friends to the wider living world of plants and animals. Most children know or learn what 'kind behaviour' looks like, and some children will be particularly sensitive in their own feelings or in their feelings towards others. However, it takes experience to internalise what kindness means, to develop empathy and compassion and to make kindness a way of life. It's only through experience and feedback that children will understand kindness at a deeper level and will be able to integrate it with their thoughts and beliefs, thereby making it their own.

Narrative

THE ROOTS OF EMPATHY

The Roots of Empathy programme was developed by Mary Gordon in Canada and has gained popularity worldwide due to growing evidence that developing empathy in young children reduced their aggression and bullying.

In the programme, children in primary schools are introduced to a human baby 'teacher' ranging from two months to four months old at the beginning of the school year. The baby makes regular visits to the class with its carer and a Roots of Empathy facilitator. Through the course of the school year, the children watch the baby grow and change. The children are asked to observe several different emotions conveyed by the baby that they might not recognise as easily in children their own age. For example, the baby may start crying and the facilitator will ask the children why the baby is crying. The teacher helps children recognise and talk about feelings in the baby and then to relate this to their own feelings and the feelings of others.

We can apply similar principles and methods when working with Early Years children outside, for example by encouraging children to get to know and care for small and tender plants or baby animals. This work can begin to sow the seeds of empathy and demonstrate the importance of kind behaviour that can grow throughout the child's life. Babies and young children can be our teachers too!

Narrative

KIM AND PEYTON: UNDERSTANDING KINDNESS IS NOT ALWAYS EASY

Some children find it harder to learn collective values or the rules of a group. Kim had a diagnosis of autism. She found it harder to understand the concept of kindness than other children in her group. She was not sure what kindness was exactly, why it was important, or how to express it the typical situations the nursery expected. She found it difficult to read the communication cues in people's body language. She needed lots of experience to understand the expectations around kindness and how her behaviour impacts on others. She needed more help in learning

how to pick up clues about other people's feelings and responses to her behaviour and how to relate them to their own experience and internal references.

Peyton also had difficulties picking up on the cues of others. He would laugh when people hurt themselves and appeared not to know the difference between when someone was laughing or crying. However, he had a natural affinity to animals. Outdoors, he related strongly to animals, built sanctuaries for insects and was brilliant at taking care of the new chicks when they hatched. His teachers and carers used these opportunities to praise his kindness and relate it to other situations.

Freedom, rights and responsibilities

The sense of freedom comes in many forms – freedom of thought, movement, action, speech and other kinds of expression. Sometimes freedom is seen as threatening to authority. Children generally have much less freedom and authority than adults. They learn early on that their freedom of movement is restricted if it is seen as endangering themselves or others. They learn what is 'against the rules'. They learn that their freedom is connected to their level of independence and skill, and is linked to responsibility. With greater freedom comes more responsibility – to take care of yourself and others. So, if they learn to put on their outdoor clothes unassisted, they may have greater freedom to choose when to go outdoors. When they have learned how to use tools safely, they will be given more freedom to use them unassisted.

On reflection

WHAT DOES FREEDOM MEAN TO YOU?

The United Nations Conventions on the Rights of the Child (articles 13, 14, 15) cites three essential rights for children regarding freedom: the freedom of thought, the freedom of speech and the freedom of association.

Here are some questions for your own reflection or to start a discussion within your team:

- What do these mean to your practice?

- What does 'being free' mean to you?

- What kinds of freedom do you value in your life and in your work?

- How do you encourage, support or restrict children's freedoms in your setting?

In practice

FREEDOM WALL

Developing ideas of liberty and freedom outdoors can take many forms. You could work with your children to develop a 'freedom wall' outside with photos of 'fun things we are free to do outdoors'. Here are some ideas to get you started:

- We are free to learn about nature and to explore our surroundings.

- We are free to move – run, jump, crawl, skip.

- We are free to talk about thing that matter to us.

- We are free to be still and to daydream.

- We are free to be alone or to play with our friends.

Children should be free to move or to be still and daydream

Fairness and consequences

Our sense of justice is related to our ideas of fairness and the appropriateness of rewards or punishments in response to different actions. It is also about equality and calling attention to the way people are different and the way people are the same, but recognising that everyone is worthy of equal respect, whatever their individual or family identity. As with the sense of freedom, there will be many interpretations and differences in what people think is fair or just. As teachers and carers, we can reflect on our own beliefs and attitudes and be open to critical challenge and learning. We can become aware of the way that our own cultural identities affect the way we teach. We can reflect with colleagues and develop shared values about how we teach and learn together.

As teachers and carers, we should be aware of what our behaviour 'says' to children about fairness. We can observe, be attentive to children's play and conversation and pick up on compelling questions, concerns or misunderstandings that arise.

A sense of justice extends not just to the human world but also to the wider ecological world. Land ownership and use and distribution of the world's resources are not evenly spread. Even at local level around you, children and families will enjoy different levels of material wealth, they will have varying experiences of and access to plants, green space, animals, and even to fresh air and sky.

Sharing resources

In practice

WORKING WITH NATURE IS A GREAT WAY TO EXPERIENCE VALUES

Outdoors is great place to practise sharing resources, thinking about what is fair and noticing the impact of our actions on other living things. We can do this by:

- Noticing what is abundant in nature and only using those resources, e.g. if we have lots of dandelions, we may pick some into make stews, perfume brews or even proper edible dandelion jam. However, if there are only a few flowers in the field or the garden, or we know they are rare we need to leave them for others to enjoy, and so they can seed themselves and come back next year.

- Sharing what we have – whether it's sticks, seeds or berry crops. When we harvest or make collections of things outdoors, there are good opportunities to learn mathematical solutions to 'fairness'. How do we measure what we each have? Are there enough for us to two or ten blackberries each?

The rules of behaviour may be determined by our thoughts about safety, but they are also often determined by our values. If children have internalised values about fairness, kindness and taking care of themselves and others, their behaviour will be 'pro-social'. For some children, this can be more difficult than others, and they may take longer to learn these behaviours. They may never internalise the values or behave in ways others want them to, no matter what the rules are or how severe the consequences.

Laws of nature, behaviour, responsibility and consequences

Nature teaches us about actions, natural laws and consequences: if we touch fire, we get burnt; if we don't water the plants or feed the fish, they die. As teachers, we can work with the children learn about what is in their control and what is not and where we need to develop responsibility around our actions. We can decide on the essential rules we need to keep ourselves and others safe outdoors. We can also experience the laws or rules of nature – things we cannot change – and the consequences of our actions through real experience of science and engineering projects. For example, we are learning about gravity when we learn to balance ourselves, when we use balance scales in the sandpit or use pipes and guttering to change the speed and direction of poured water. If we have a fire, we can observe combustion and discover what happens when we burn different kind of materials – hay, paper, wood, charcoal – and the effect of wind on fire.

Equality, tolerance and mutual respect

There has been a huge amount of national legislation and global policy making around equality. Inequality, prejudice, stereotyping and discrimination are the basis on which many wars have been fought and many injustices have been done. Children develop their values around equality, their stereotypes and prejudices very early. As teachers working outdoors, we have many opportunities to encourage children to think about equality and other values, question their assumptions and allow them to question ours. We might think that 'boys need to get outside to let off steam' or that girls 'don't like to get dirty'. We even have a famous nursery rhyme about boys being made of 'slugs and snails and puppy dogs tails' and girls being made of 'sugar and spice and all things nice'. We may inadvertently praise qualities of courage, active play and adventure in boys, and more nurturing and aesthetic qualities in girls. Gender stereotypes are perhaps some of the earliest ones to be formed in our culture. In many retail outlets, even outdoor clothing is gender biased – pink and flimsy for girls, blue and tough for boys.

Boys and girls deserve equal opportunities to develop all their capacities and use all the resources

On reflection

BOYS AND GIRLS COME OUT TO PLAY

If you want to read about the early lives of some of our most famous women naturalists (there are far fewer famous women naturalists than men) look at *Girls Who Looked Under Rocks* by Jennine Atkins. Early experiences outdoors will foster a scientific interest in nature in girls as well as boys – if only they are encouraged to see their explorations as valued, purposeful and enjoyable activities.

Think about:

- What do you do to encourage girls into scientific explorations outdoors? Do they get involved building and engineering projects in the sandpit, or with construction tasks?

- What do you do to encourage boys to get involved in nurturing tasks outdoors, e.g. taking care of plants and animals? Do they get involved in more sensory activities such as making perfumes or petal garlands?

If you are working with a class or group of boys and girls, it is useful to do regular observations of your outdoor space and take regular snapshots of how different spaces are used. Are some spaces used more by boys than by girls? Ask the children why they think this might be the case. What would they like to do about it?

A sense of place

Depending on where they live and are brought up, young children will encounter varying cultural beliefs around nature, the outdoors and dirt. Some families may have spiritual or supernatural beliefs about nature. Many traditional stories talk about witches, ghosts, jinns or ogres that live in the woods. Most faiths also have festivals that celebrate nature's gifts at harvest – often involving food or gifts.

In practice

EQUAL BUT DIFFERENT

Sometimes it is in the little things that show our values. As teachers, we need to consider the choices we make about the equipment or food we provide and what value messages the children are picking up from our choices – both what we do provide and what we leave out.

- If you provide outdoor clothing for children, focus on quality and function for both boys and girls and encourage parents to do the same. All children can wear all colours.

- Find out about celebrations and food eaten by the families of your children. Can you celebrate any of them outdoors, and can you make connections between the food and where it is grown?

Tread carefully around other peoples' beliefs. Offer non-judgemental responses and encourage positive dispositions towards nature. Give children opportunities to talk about any fears, and how to manage them. Talk about the different ways we all celebrate and give thanks for things we appreciate. Avoid getting sucked in to 'taking sides' when children disagree, or 'correcting' the beliefs they bring with them. You can say 'different people have different beliefs about that. What do you believe?'.

Purpose

A sense of purpose is linked to motivation and having aspirations or goals. When we observe babies and young children, they seem to have an innate sense of purpose – they 'go about their business' of exploration of the world around them with single-mindedness and determination. As teachers and carers, we make the most of children's innate curiosity and desire to try out new things. Some adult behaviours can dampen or even destroy children's sense of purpose early on. Telling babies and toddlers 'no' too often can make them lose motivation or get overwhelmed with frustration. Restricting movement or constantly interrupting the flow of their play by distracting them or asking unnecessary questions can 'switch off' the neural pathways associated with purpose and the desire to learn. Of course, we sometimes need to say no to prevent babies and young children from causing themselves serious harm but allowing them to take some risks is important for learning. A culture where making mistakes is acceptable is important if children are to gain confidence rather than lose heart when things go wrong.

Overly-helpful adults can also prevent children's sense of purpose – their agency, natural drive and confidence to 'have a go'. Children are fascinated by adults' sense of purpose and want to join in purposeful tasks. This sense of apprenticeship in the Early Years, through joining in with tasks that have purpose and are valued by others, is the beginning of citizenship and stewardship: the beginning of taking responsibility and caring for others and the Earth.

Agency and purpose

On reflection

PURPOSE, APPRENTICESHIP AND STEWARDSHIP

As teachers and carers, we can positively respond to and help children develop their sense of purpose outdoors by:

- giving children time and space to follow their curiosity and desire to explore.

- encouraging children's agency through attention, attunement and sensitivity about when to assist or intervene in a child's endeavours and when not to interfere.

- having a positive attitude to mistakes or minor accidents which happen when we 'have a go' or try something new.

- encouraging children through 'companionable helping' or apprenticeship tasks where they do practical things alongside the adults in order to care for others or the environment.

- talking about and valuing the work and sense of purpose of others, e.g. the gardener, the delivery people, or the road or building construction workers in your street.

In practice

DEVELOPING A SENSE OF PURPOSE OUTDOORS – APPRENTICESHIP

You can encourage a sense of purpose in a number of ways when working outdoors if you:

- involve children in adult led tasks such as planting, watering, or tidying up.

- support children to manage tasks that either you or they initiate, e.g. transporting water; digging, sifting, raking soil; picking food crops; constructing or building things; taking care of nature by feeding the birds.

- respond to child-initiated efforts by praising what they are doing rather than the end product, and by encouraging and showing appreciation and gratitude. You might praise their perseverance in a construction project, their skill in sweeping up sand, or their kindness in sharing the berries they have just picked.

Apprenticeship tasks – there are always plenty of ways to help outside

On reflection

WHAT COMPUTERS CANNOT DO

So many things can be done more quickly with technology these days – counting, calculating, sharing information, and ideas with others. As we increasingly make use of the wonders of technology, let's also pause and think what computers cannot do or teach so we make sure that there is plenty of room for this too. Computers can teach 'about' values as abstract concepts with examples, but they cannot teach children the felt sense of gratitude when receiving a gift from a close friend. They cannot teach the direct gratification of how a plant flourishes and grows when it is watered, or how an animal responds when it is stroked. Those experiences teach responsibility and reciprocity and about the preciousness of life. Computers cannot offer opportunities to learn things like kindness, purpose or connection as lived and embodied experience. Technological developers are exploring how to make technology appeal to more of our sense doorways – smell and touch, for example. They are also exploring how technology can support sense windows of balance, orientation and movement – particularly for rehabilitation. Technology is currently no match for teaching through experience outdoors.

In what ways might you use technology together with outdoor experience for added value? Can you think of ways that computers can teach any of your values better than real experience outdoors?

Connection

> 'It is in such profound instinctive union with the stream of life that the greatest joy is to be found.'
>
> Bertrand Russell

Connection is about relationships and whether we feel 'in touch' with others. It can also be a connection to place and whether we feel we belong and have a feeling of being 'at home'. Connection can be an internal felt sense of integration, a sense of wholeness of mind and body and spirit, or even a feeling of 'oneness' with the whole of the world. Bertrand Russell describes how, if we truly take an interest in other persons or things outside ourselves, we become 'part of the stream of life', not separate from it like a billiard ball which simply collides with other billiard balls. When we feel connected, we feel like citizens of the universe, enjoying what it offers, and are not troubled so much by thoughts of what will become of us in the future.

Perhaps the most fundamental connection for young children is their attachment to parents or other primary caregivers, and there has been much research about the damage that can be done if those attachments are disrupted or not given a chance to flourish. As teachers and carers, we can observe how connected children feel by their behaviour, whether they seem 'comfortable in their skin' and by what Ferre Laevers terms 'linkedness'. In Chapter 7, we explore how this sense of connection can be accessed through beauty, awe and wonder, through gratitude and appreciation, and through nurturing the roots of resilience.

Further reading

To find out more about the ideas in this chapter, search online for:

- ✿ 'The 12 principles of permaculture' by David Holmgren
- ✿ The 'Think Equal' charity
- ✿ Erin Kenny on the 'Cedarsong Forest Kindergarten'
- ✿ Ferre Laevers on 'linkedness'
- ✿ Mary Gordon on the 'Roots of Empathy'
- ✿ Monica Edwards' book, *Global Childhoods*
- ✿ David Orr on 'Earth mindedness'.

Connection to each other and to nature

A sense of place

Mindfulness pedagogy in the Early Years

> 'Slow down and enjoy life. It's not only the scenery you miss by going too fast – you also miss the sense of where you are going and why.'
>
> Eddie Cantor

Chapter overview

This chapter introduces mindfulness to those who are new to it and offers some practical ways in which it can be applied in Early Years' practice. Connecting with nature using our sense doorways, sense windows and sense skylights is a way in to mindfulness practice and mindful pedagogy. This chapter offers resources to support you on a journey towards becoming more fully present, more relaxed and mindful in your work with young children.

Key ideas

✿ What is mindful pedagogy?

✿ Mindfulness – origins and sources

✿ Being too busy and not having enough time

✿ The four A's of mindful pedagogy: awareness, attention, attunement and affordance

What is mindful pedagogy?

When we slow down, become fully present and attentive to young children's moment-by-moment curiosities and interests, it makes a hugely positive difference to the quality of their play and learning. As teachers of young children, you know how difficult it can be to stay in that fully present and attentive 'zone' when there are so many other demands on your time. So how can you change things? How can you make more time to be more relaxed and focused and to stay 'in flow' with the children in your work? There is significant research evidence of the benefits of mindfulness practice for better mental health and wellbeing, reduced stress and for increased cognitive functioning and focus.

Mindful pedagogy is all about making things simpler, more focused, and less busy or distracted. But this is not always easy to achieve right away. Like most things, the more you practise, the easier and more natural it feels.

Mindfulness is about making things simpler and more focused – taking out the stress

Mindfulness – origins and sources

The aim of mindfulness practice is help us to have more peaceful, more balanced, more joyful and more meaningful lives. By allowing this to affect the way we behave in our everyday lives, mindfulness also aims to support others to have more peace, balance and joy in their lives. Mindfulness is thought to have its origins in Buddhist philosophy and practice, although many other traditions and cultures have similar meditation-type practices that aim to create greater calm within us and more peace and kindness in the wider world. Mindfulness can be practised whatever your background and beliefs are – by anyone of any faith or religion and those who do not subscribe to any religion at all.

The two best-known, formalised approaches to mindfulness developed in recent years in the western world are Mindfulness-Based Stress Reduction (MBSR) and Mindfulness-Based Cognitive Therapy (MBCT), both of which are taught over a number of sessions and are completely secular in nature.

In the USA, Jon Kabat-Zinn and his colleagues developed Mindfulness-Based Stress Reduction and in the UK, Professor Mark Williams and team have developed Mindfulness-Based Cognitive Therapy. Both programmes are recognised by health and education bodies, and mindfulness courses are now widely available. Mindfulness techniques are now also often included in other training courses and programmes that aim to enable people to stabilise and balance their lives, reduce stress and stop their mind 'running away with them'.

If you do not already have a meditation or mindfulness practice and you want to learn more, it can be a good idea to attend a course, after which you can practise on your own or join a regular group. Some Early Years' settings introduce mindfulness as part of their professional development and build it into their routines for the week and the way they work.

Being too busy and not having enough time

'It is possible to live happily in the here and now. So many conditions of happiness are available — more than enough for you to be happy right now. You don't have to run into the future in order to get more.'

Thich Nhat Hanh

'We don't have enough time and the workload is too much!' This the constant cry of many practitioners. The one thing we never seem to have enough of is time. Our lives are full of things we feel we should or must do – paperwork, emails, records, assessments, meetings, training – and that is just at work! Our home lives may also be full of the pressures of 'life laundry' from paying bills to shopping or planning a night out or a holiday. Technology has enabled us to do much of this faster – or has it? How many hours do we spend on forgotten passwords, updating our software and devices, downloading new apps? We can spend a whole morning on circular phone calls to sort out a problem with an order or a bill or dealing with a technical glitch or major fault that needs sorting.

It seems there is no escape from being 'plugged in'. Technology has brought many gifts and enabled us to keep in contact with relatives – even when they live far away. It has enabled us to mine information faster and to connect in new ways. It has also created new expectations about response time and keeping in touch. For example, in early years and childcare settings, parents may have expectations about how they receive information about their children using new electronic records and newsletters. Updating websites, Facebook pages and electronic records have been added to the list of essential tasks for many early years settings.

The funny thing about time is that the more squeezed we feel and the more pressure we are under, the more time seems to run away from us, like grains of sand in an egg timer. When we slow down, take the pressure off and become more fully 'in' the present moment, then our sense of the time we have can expand and become more spacious. Mindfulness can help us connect with the sense of spaciousness and present moment focus.

Mindfulness is not about filling up our mind. Indeed, it is almost the opposite – creating more space. Maybe it could be better named 'mind clarification'. Consider a glass of muddy water full of sediment from the pond. If it is left for a few hours of stillness, it will become clearer as the sediment sinks to the bottom of the glass. It can be like that for our minds: when the sediment of our everyday thoughts, or 'mind chatter', settles our minds can clear a little – giving us greater capacity to focus, prioritise and work more efficiently and effectively.

A sense of place

The four As: awareness, attention, attunement and affordance

Awareness

Awareness comes from simply noticing where we are right now – and how we feel – using our sense doorways. What is going on in my body? What is happening with my breath? Where am I right now? What is going on around me? What can I see, hear, smell? Am I tense or relaxed? What's the weather like today? What is happening in nature this season? How noisy or quiet are the children? Where is my energy? Where is the energy in the others in the room?

Attention

Attention comes from focusing in on what is needed right now: What is needed in my body? Am I thirsty and do I need to drink? Am I feeling tense and should I drop my shoulders, wriggle my fingers or take a deep breath? Have I been rushing around, and do I need to sit down? Have I been sitting in one spot, getting stiff and need to move around? What are the children around me doing? Where am I most needed right now?

Listening to a mindfulness chime outside

Attunement

Attunement is about aligning your attention with that of another. This means using all your senses to 'feel into' what is going on for a particular child, or groups of children, at any moment. It relies on your ability to pick up on non-verbal clues (see sense windows in Chapter 4) and the capacity to 'see' the world from the point of view of the child. What are they thinking and feeling right now? What are they curious about? How are they expressing themselves? What do they need now? Attunement is also about sensing the environment and what is needed. What needs clearing and where would additional resources serve better? What does that animal or insect or plant need now in order to flourish? What does the fire need to burn better?

Affordance

'Affordance' was a term introduced in Chapter 3, described as the invitations and possibilities that environmental features or objects offer us. Affordances allow or invite us to react in different ways according to our abilities, capacities and inclinations. Affordance is relevant to mindful pedagogy because it encourages us to notice the resources around us – to stop, look and listen – before we respond. In any outside environment, nature 'affords' us so much variety. What is going on with the weather right now? Is it a day to learn about shadows or the properties of ice? What is happening in the season right now? Is it time to learn about butterflies or acorns? What materials are abundant right now?

In practice

THE MINDFULNESS CHIME – CREATING A PAUSE OR AWARENESS IN WHICH TO STOP AND BREATHE

The practice of using a chime or bell to call other people to attention is certainly not new in education. A mindfulness chime can create pauses in a busy day – an opportunity to refocus.

A mindfulness chime needs to have a beautiful tone – usually a single note from a 'singing bowl' or chime bar that reverberates for a long time. You can find a wide range for sale on the Internet.

When we hear the mindfulness chime, it is an invitation to stop whatever we are doing and to notice how we are right now in our bodies. When you start using the bell, you might want to think 'stop, breathe, notice'. With children, you might encourage them to think 'stop, breathe, listen':

1. Stop

In those moments after the you hear the bell, quickly scan through your different body parts – from head, through legs, trunk, neck, and head – noticing any areas of tension and consciously relaxing them.

2. Breathe

Notice how you are breathing. Where is your breath? Breathe a little more fully. Become aware of what is going on around you.

3. Notice/Listen

Check in with your sense doorways: what can you see, hear, smell? What is going around you?

These three stages can take a few moments only. Then a second sounding of the chime tells us to carry on and re-engage with our activities, tasks or interactions – but with greater awareness and attention.

BABIES AND TODDLERS

If you work with babies and toddlers, it will be the adult carers that respond to the bell at first. Slowly the babies and children will learn the change in atmosphere that happens when the chime goes – and they will respond accordingly.

OLDER CHILDREN

When introducing the mindful bell to older children, you can teach them to say to themselves 'stop, breathe, look, listen'. Encourage them to use their sense doorways: eyes, ears, feet and hands to notice what is going on right now. Ask them to raise their hand when they no longer hear the sound reverberating, which will fade very slowly.

GETTING STARTED

When you first start using the mindfulness bell it may seem disruptive and awkward. Experiment with the length of pause that works well for your team, children and setting. Practise it with the children at group time first. Members of staff can take it turns to chime the bell at regular intervals throughout the day – maybe once an hour or less frequently. When you hear the bell, you might say aloud 'stop, breathe, notice' and the children will learn to do the same. It is a bit like musical statues, but children must remember to breathe as well as well as be still. However, unlike musical statues there is no competition or getting it wrong!

A sense of place

Focusing on breath

One of the key ways into mindfulness practice is learning to use our breath. If we slow down and focus on how we are breathing, this can help us direct our attention better. A baby or young child will pick up on your breathing as you hold them. They will know whether you are calm, anxious or upset. Breathing gently and slowly with long exhales will slow your heart rate and make you calmer. Focusing on our breath can also help us to calm down and become more present.

This book focuses on the opportunities working with nature and outdoors can bring. However, there are now many resources available more generally to support mindfulness with children, including exercises which help practitioners and children use their breath for calming. You can also find suggestions for further reading at the end of this chapter.

The rocking rhythm of a hammock can be very soothing

Noticing breath – blowing

In practice

FINDING RHYTHM (BABIES AND CHILDREN UNDER TWO)

Children under two are not conscious of their breath but they will notice your breathing. If they are upset and you hold them and slow your breathing, they will pick up on this and it will help them calm down. They are used to the sounds of the womb and their mothers' heartbeat; the sounds of nature can recreate something similar, as can the sound of your voice or your body clapping gently or drumming. Taking children outside often has the immediate effect of calming babies and toddlers. Rocking and singing, using rhymes whilst walking around under the sky. If you happen to be near the sea, the rhythm of the waves can echo the rhythm of the breath. If you are near a forest or tall trees, the sound of the breeze in the leaves can create a similar calming effect. If you have enough space, a hammock can be a lovely resource for carers and young children to lie in and rock – creating natural rhythm of swinging, humming, singing together.

In practice

NATURE'S BREATH – ACTIVITIES WITH WIND AND AIR THROUGH THE SEASONS

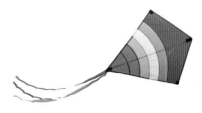

Helping children become aware of their breath can help them to calm their thoughts and feelings when needed. Breath can help them slow down, cool down and pay attention to their bodies, their environment and things around them. Different seasons bring different opportunities for engaging sense doorways and working with the breeze – nature's breath.

1. Listen

Wind chimes with beautiful sounds are a great way of using the sense doorway of sound to notice what is happening with the invisible breath of the wind. Choose high-quality wind chimes with sounds that you enjoy, preferably with different tones. With older children, you can make your own out of sticks, shells with holes and other found materials.

2. Look up

In warmer weather, most babies and toddlers will enjoy just lying under a tree and watching the interplay of leaves and light. Make sure they are warm enough. Some babies prefer to be wrapped up, some are happy to kick freely, and some need move between the two. Take walks to places where children can look up and see trees.

3. Frosty breath

Frosty winter days are a great time for exploring breath as we can see it as visible steam coming out of our mouths. Play with seeing how long you can make your breath. Can you do little puffs? Cold day 'smoky' breath can also be used to melt ice on window panes and to blow bubbles if you have a bubble blowing kit.

4. Blowing seeds

In summer days, if you are lucky enough to have dandelions around, children will use their breath to blow the seeds around. Sycamore seeds in autumn make great little propellers when dropped from a height to be carried in the wind.

5. Cool down

Children who have become overheated from running around can be encouraged to find a shady spot and do 'cool down breathing': in through your nose and then long out through your mouth. Or, placing your hands on your tummy, try to breathe into your tummy so you 'fill it up from the inside' like a balloon, and then slowly let it down as you breathe the air out again.

6. Fly a kite

This is most fun as children get older. Flying kites requires a lot of presence and in-the-moment mindfulness – feeling the wind through the string and focusing on keeping it in the air. Children under six or seven will probably need an adult to help them get the kite in the air – and you need a day that has just the right amount of wind – not too strong and not too weak – blowing steadily. For happy kite flying, you really need a wide-open space to run around, also allowing enough space for the kite to come down again without getting tangled in trees, people or other objects in the landscape.

In practice

WORKING WITH FIRE

Children are fascinated by candles and they create a sense of stillness and celebration. They quickly become aware that flames are hot and must not be touched so they need to slow down and be careful. If they blow on a candle, or rush past, the candle can go out.

Try having a still time with a candle in the centre of a circle, or next to the teacher at story time. See what difference it makes to behaviour, mood and heightened awareness to the present moment. Children over three will enjoy taking it in turns to blow the candle out.

There is nothing like a real fire for focusing attention. You can now get fire bowls in all sizes, which are safe to use in almost any outdoor space. Of course, it is important to introduce fire making and sitting around a fire to children carefully and in stages. Even very young babies will enjoy seeing a fire burn and watching the way the smoke blows while sitting safely on someone's lap. Older children, beyond three years, can be involved in the process of building and lighting a fire from scratch. They will learn that breath can also help fire burn more quickly. Blowing on the fire through bellows or a blow pipe can help further.

Narrative

JESS: FIRE STORIES

Before becoming a nursery teacher, Jess used to work in an adventure playground for children aged five to 15. A central part of their daily provision was a fire pit, which burned most of the time the adventure playground was open. The children quickly learned the few rules: never run or shove by the fire; only burn wood and paper. The playworkers ensured there were fire buckets full of water present, and there was on-going risk assessment about the level of supervision required, depending on which children were in and how busy they were. The fire pit was a place of sitting and talking, watching the flames, gently stoking and sometimes cooking and sharing food. It was a place to tell stories because children naturally settled down around the fire and became more still.

When she moved to teach in an Early Years setting, Jess wanted to recreate a similar atmosphere and to introduce fire to the children from a very young age. Unlike at the adventure playground, constant supervision was needed, and it was necessary to spend more time on teaching the children to walk around the outside of the 'fire ring' of log seats – not inside.

The children responded very well – learning how to find kindling and fold newspaper into paper 'doughnuts' for easy lighting. They learned to take care not to get burned – and indeed this usually only happened when they were too quick to eat their fire-cooked bread without pausing to give it enough time to cool down.

Working with fire

Savouring slowness and being still

Slowing down and making observations from a child's-eye view can help us notice what each child is interested in doing right now. Stillness is a rare quality these days, but one that we can cultivate with practise. Spontaneity is important if we are to make the most of the opportunities presented to us. This is particularly important outdoors, when we might need to change even the best-laid plans because of the weather.

Young children learn naturally by moving and exploring their surroundings. Sitting still is an unlikely occupation for most children in their Early Years. They are learning to use their bodies, build their muscles, follow their curiosities and discover new things. However, adults are always rushing about – except maybe when glued in front of a screen. Primary school teachers in particular may often complain that children come to school unable to sit still. This is probably because they are not developmentally ready to sit still – they are too busy learning how to move. However, it may also be that they just don't know about sitting still and what this might look like or feel like. How can we expect them to learn the value of sitting still when the adults around them don't do it? They see adults rushing around doing stuff, responding to stuff, being busy. If we, as adults, value stillness so little, why should children think it is something to try or to aspire to?

Sitting still in nature helps us notice the invitations or affordances that nature offers for learning and the impact this can have on our own wellbeing as well that of the children.

On reflection

FINDING YOUR SIT SPOT

Ask yourself: When do children see you sitting still – not doing anything except being aware and noticing with eyes and ears? When do your children ever see anyone sitting still? Keep a mental note or log of whether this happens at any point of the day in your work.

A sit spot is any place where you can sit and totally relax and be still. Sit spot practice is finding a place – or several places – where you can do this regularly. By visiting the same place often, you become familiar with it and relax more quickly. By practising sitting still regularly, you learn to calm your mind and become more focused. Doing this in nature is particularly wonderful because you can use the sights and sounds to help you focus and settle; you can often breathe more deeply and be restored by nature around you. Even quite young children enjoy sit spot practice. But young children's key learning involves movement and they should never be required to sit still for any extended period.

It is a good idea to develop your own sit spot practice before you introduce it to others. Find time to simply sit still once a while. Not 'zoning out' but 'tuning in' to what is going on inside you and around you. This is great preparation for better child observations and developing awareness and attunement.

- Find a place outdoors where you are really comfortable and can feel relaxed. This should be a place that feels good to you – it might be your doorstep or a park bench, a piece of ground under a tree or on a rock on a beach.

- As soon as you sit you can think to yourself, stop, breathe, smell, look, listen and feel. Take deep, gentle breathes and 'check in' with yourself. There is nothing to do right now other than 'just be'. Visit your sit spot regularly just to practise.

In a nursery or other Early Years setting, find a sit spot you enjoy in the garden or outdoor area and spend a few minutes just noticing. You are not 'doing an observation' but you will notice a lot which can feed into your observations and planning.

Remember: if we sit still sometimes, it can help children see and recognise the value of stillness.

A sense of place

In practice

SIT SPOTS WITH CHILDREN

You can practise using sit spots with very young children and even babies. They will quickly notice the different quality of your attention during sit spot practise. Around the age of three and half (or younger or older depending on their developmental stage), children can begin regular 'sit spot practice' with you or in a group.

1. In a group, give each child a square of carpet, a piece of foam carry mat or a cushion with waterproof backing.

2. Each child should choose their own sit spot. They might need a little while to decide. It can be helpful to ask the children to find a sit spot for a favourite teddy. Where would teddy be comfortable? Which area would he like to sit in? What can he see from here do you think? What can he smell? What can he hear? Can you show teddy what to do? Ask the children to sit on their cushion and stop, breathe, look, listen.

3. Start with just a minute or two of sit spot practice. As the children get used to it, you can extend the time. Some children will take to it straight away, others may find it more challenging. Don't emphasise stillness if children find this difficult. Just gently encourage children to breathe, look and listen quietly.

4. Collect children from their sit spots and bring them together to talk about how they felt and what they noticed in their sit spot today. At first, they may need prompting: How was your sit spot today? How do you feel? Did anyone see or hear anything special interesting? A bird? An insect? What was going on with the trees today? This is a good way of starting circle time.

Finding a good sit spot can help children to focus and improve their attention

Narrative

ISOBEL: SIT SPOTS FOR STAFF AT PLAYGROUP

When Isobel introduced sit spots in her setting, she encouraged staff to take turns to have 'sit spot' time in the garden. Each morning, a different member of staff had their turn at 'sit spotting' instead of setting up and preparing for the children with the rest of the team. They found it 'a bit weird' to begin with, but after some time they looked forward to their sit spot morning. It was a time for them to consciously relax after the rush to get up and get to work. They noticed that they became more conscious of what was happening with the weather, the season and in the environment. Paying greater attention to scents and sounds outdoors gave them good ideas about how to expand the way they used resources, and their possibilities for children. As they became more used to the practice, they found it really helped them to clear their minds and focus, improving their attention and the quality of the observations they made.

Spontaneous and seasonal responses to the affordances of nature

Being in nature can be a big support to mindfulness practice. There are increasing number of wellbeing programmes that combine mindfulness and being outdoors. Your environment and the seasons will determine what kind of resources you are able to draw on. You might be near big trees, the beach or a river. You might have big views and a wide horizon, or you may have to focus more closely on the plants and insects that make their homes in the cracks of pavements or public parks.

We are part of nature and nature is always around us wherever we are. In parts of the world with temperate climates, we get a greater variety of weather throughout the year than in more tropical zones. The landscape, plants and trees reveal themselves to us in changing glory. There are piles of leaves or conkers or seeds to revel in autumn; banks of daffodils, bluebells and wild garlic and in spring; and sunflowers and daisy chains in summer. We have changing food crops in fields, orchards and hedges. We have plenty of water wherever we are and can taste the rain or feel the warmth of the sun, see shadows lengthen and shorten depending on the time of day and the season. As practitioners, you can notice what is abundant each day and support the children to notice this too. But nature is not always predictable, so planning needs plenty of flexibility to respond to spontaneous invitations – rainbows, piles of leaves blown in by the gale or the magical appearance of icicles or snow.

Use what nature provides each season

Narrative

SPONTANEOUS RESPONSES TO SNOW

Chris and her team had a plan for the week that was all about birds. Chris had bought some new birdseed feeders and hung them from hooks on a pole outside the window. It was February and the children had shown an interest in the increasing number of birds that were visiting. Chris thought that this week they would make their own bird feeders and get more books about birds on the discovery table.

On Monday morning, it snowed. The arrival of snow was unusual enough for all plans to be thrown out. Snow creates a total change in the environment and requires a spontaneous plan. How beautiful and pristine the snow looked with the sun sparkling on it. Before they even went outside, Chris looked at the awe and excitement on the children's faces: 'It glitters. There's ice!'. When they went outside, they noticed the sound was different too – everything was a bit muffled. They noticed tracks. What made them? That day and the next was filled with discovery of the 'affordances' of snow: it's good for transporting, building and making tracks, trails and snowballs to throw. At the end of the day, the children helped Chris fill a tuff tray with water and polar creatures that created an ice landscape the next morning. They filled balloons with water and left them outside to make 'ice balls'. The birds were still very much part of the picture that week; footprints were a new line of enquiry, and bird feeders were made. However, the focus of the week was different – the highlight was the quality of snow and how it changed everything, the awe and wonder, the excitement and laughter that it produced.

A sense of place

Companionship learning

> 'If a child is to keep his inborn sense of wonder, he needs the companionship of at least one adult who can share it, rediscovering with him (or her) the joy, excitement, and mystery of the world we live in.'
>
> Rachel Carson

In Early Years, we talk about adult-initiated and child-initiated learning and both of these concepts are useful. Companionship learning is a three-way connection between adult, child and the environment. When we learn alongside children, attuned to their needs and to the environment, learning flows in a kind of dance or like a game of ping pong.

> '"Anchored companionship" with a child is one of the greatest gifts we can give. These are times when children know you won't go away.'
>
> Rosemary Roberts

Teachers can be companions in learning with their children by sensitively responding to their play 'cues' or invitations to explore, engage, interact, play and learn.

We can hold a container of awareness, presence and attention in which children's learning and development can respond to the environment and flourish in its own unique way.

Practitioner

Nature

Child

Narrative

MAITE: ME, YOU AND NATURE – A COMPANIONSHIP WALK

Maite and her childminder are out for a walk. It is autumn and they are walking through the park. There are lot of golden leaves on the ground. Suddenly, a gust of wind stirs some of the leaves and Maite laugh and runs along with them. Her childminder responds to her 'cue' and the invitation of the leaves. The childminder picks up a handful of leaves and throws them in the air to catch the wind. Maite laughs even more and picks up some leaves and throws them too.

The four elements – Maite, her childminder, the leaves and the wind continue in an extended playful dance for many minutes. Maite is fully engaged and joyful. She is stretching her whole body and tests her strength to see how far and how high she can throw the leaves, she enjoys the sensation of the leaves falling on her head and is discovering something about the properties of air, leaves and breeze as she plays.

Her childminder is attuned to both Maite and the environment; she is noticing Maite's development – where she moves with ease and where she struggles with direction and mobility. She initiates new movements – such as kicking the leaves. She is thinking about what other experiences Maite might enjoy – tasting the rain? Flying a kite? This is a learning journey of equality and companionship. It is almost impossible to say whether this extended interaction is child initiated, adult initiated, or initiated by the affordance offered by nature in the form of the fallen autumn leaves and the wind.

Companionship learning

Appreciating beauty and awakening gratitude

Beauty is in the eye of the beholder they say, and how do we train those eyes to notice and appreciate? We can miss the moments if we are not closely paying attention, and if we don't respond to and honour the moment that a child is affected by the beauty of something – a rainbow in dew drop, a squirrel running up a tree, the rising moon or the setting sun. Children learn that such things are commonplace when their exclamations of awe are not met by responses from their companions. This may mean that the surprises of nature can become commonplace and we lose the capacity to be awake to the wonders of our immediate surroundings – and of the planet we live on. Allowing time to stop and stare and breathe in your surroundings is part of slowing down and becoming mindful. It helps us to appreciate what we have and what we can be grateful for and happy about. Being mindful and awakening awe, wonder and gratitude is explored in more detail in the chapter about sense skylights (Chapter 5).

Moments of awe and wonder

In practice

SKY WATCHING AND WOW MOMENTS

SKY WATCHING

If you live or work in the city, you may often get limited views of the sky.

1. Lie on blanket with children and watching the shapes on a cloudy day.

2. Walk up a hill to see how much more sky you can see.

3. Take every opportunity you can get to watch the sun rise or set.

4. Take every opportunity to notice the stars and the moon (you may have a young astronomer or astronaut in your midst!).

WOW MOMENTS

Use spontaneous observations by children, e.g. the beauty of flower, the rainbow, the frost on the glass, to stop and acknowledge that observation and share it with other children. Draw attention to beauty – but give space for children to 'drink it in' before over-explaining or exclaiming.

Further reading

To find out more about the ideas in this chapter, search online for:

✿ Kabat Zinn on 'mindfulness-based stress reduction'

✿ Thich Nhat Hanh's book, *A Handful of Quiet*

✿ Rosemary Roberts' book, *Wellbeing from Birth*, especially the chapter on 'companionable learning'

✿ Martin Maudsley and Stuart Lester on 'playing out and affordances'

✿ Relax kids (www.relaxkids.com)

✿ 'Mindfulness in the Early Years'

✿ Rachel Carson's book, *A Sense of Wonder*.

Roots of resilience – a systemic approach

> 'If we surrendered to earth's intelligence
> we could rise up rooted, like trees.'
>
> Rainer Maria Rilke

Chapter overview

Our job is to give children what they need grow and flourish. The environment and the responses you give them in their early years are critical. Like young plants, they need good soil as well as appropriate nutrients and care in order to grow strong roots and to be able to weather any storms which may come their way in life. This chapter is about resilience in you, your team and particularly in the children you work with right now. It looks at the key ingredients for building resilience and explores some ideas that can support your reflections and your practice towards resilience through connection to nature.

Key ideas

✿ Being and becoming: what we want for children

✿ Resilience for you as teacher and carer

✿ Resilience in children – a systemic view

✿ The four G's: gateways to nature, connection and resilience

✿ Resilience in your workplace

Being and becoming: what we want for children

We all want our children to grow up hardy and healthy, to be happy, confident, open hearted and ready to meet the world and all that awaits them. We want resilient and resourceful children who will survive and thrive in the world as they grow. We wish them to grow up feeling at home in their bodies and comfortable in their skin. We hope our children will learn to think on their feet and make good decisions. We want them to develop the skills they need to feed, clothe and protect themselves from danger, to be independent, resourceful and creative. We want them to know contentment, joy and to be able to connect with others. We know our children need to be able to breathe fresh air, to eat healthy food and know where it comes from, and to feel safe when they go outside.

Resilience is about joy in life

Resilience enables us to adapt and learn through change, to face difficulty and bounce back with our essential wellbeing intact, and potentially even be strengthened by it.

The world is changing fast. It is full of progress and also of uncertainty and complexity.

- Parents have more consumer choices for everything – baby equipment, toys, pre-prepared food, childcare, electronic devices and entertainment.

- We have more information at our finger tips, more sources of advice and support.

- Many of us are wealthier, more informed, better entertained and live longer than previous generations.

- We have seen amazing new breakthroughs in medicine and technology and have with better healthcare.

- We have more choice in what we eat and how we work. Technology has enabled us to connect with like-minded people across former barriers of geography, language and culture.

But in our rapidly developing societies, there are also fault lines and disconnects that open up for many children and families that may become physical, emotional, social and spiritual crises.

- There is a year-on-year rise in the number of children identified as having difficulties with communication and interactions.

- There are an increasing number of prescriptions being made for mental health medications for children and young people, as well as for new mothers.

- There are growing concerns about the number of children who are overweight or have allergies, asthma and diabetes.

- Many of us are 'plugged in' to an information and communication network for many hours of the day and night through multiple devices, e.g. mobile phones, computers, tablets. Most children spend hours of each day in front of screens.

- More children in the world live in cities than in rural areas now – many of them with no gardens and little access to green space. There are environmental pressures on the quality of air, water and food we eat.

- Older generations mourn the loss of free time and outdoor play in childhood today when compared with their own childhoods.

- As more people migrate and move into cities for work, many young families experience a sense of isolation and lack of extended family and community support.

Even with all these challenges, every day the world is also full of small and large acts of human kindness and courage.

Resilience for you as a teacher and carer

Research from different disciplines has identified some 'core ingredients' of resilience. A model developed by Milly Sinclair, Amaragita Pearse and Annie Davy has drawn these strands together to create a holistic 'resilience wheel' through which you can consider your own resilience. We have also adapted it for teams and for children in the Early Years so you can use the wheel as a practical tool for mapping your current resilience. You can use the wheel for reflecting on your strengths and what you already do to support your resilience, as well as what you might want to do to protect or enhance it.

The Resilience wheel © Routes to Resilience

On reflection

YOUR RESILIENCE WHEEL

On a blank piece of paper, make a copy of the resilience wheel template (see above). Fill in each segment to the level that reflects your current level of satisfaction with that aspect of your resilience. Read the next sections and work through the reflective questions for anywhere that you feel you have scored yourself 'lower', i.e. the segment is less full. Think of two or three actions for each area that you think will help you to develop that area. If you are stuck, complete this exercise with a trusted friend or colleague. Ask for them to help you work out some actions.

Consider doing this as team to look at the team dimensions of resilience. For more information, search online for 'Routes to Resilience'.

A sense of place

Vitality and flow

Vitality and flow are subtle body energies that are engaged when we are fully immersed in things that give us energy and joy. Look at Chapter 4 on sense windows which is about subtle senses and values. These are strongly linked to this area of resilience which is all about opportunities for deep-level learning, developing confidence, competence and self-esteem. It is about enjoying what you are doing to the point where you can 'wallow' or 'lose yourself' in the flow.

On reflection

VITALITY AND FLOW

If you are bored and lack vitality and flow at work much of the time, do something about it! You could:

- Look for opportunities to engage your creativity, rather than looking for problems.

- Keep learning new things that take you out of your comfort zone.

- Do more things that you are good at and enjoy.

- Spend more time being active or sitting still outdoors. Perhaps go for a walk, a run or a wild swim.

As a team, think about:

- How can we create space to celebrate success as a team and have fun?

- When are we doing our best work as a team?

Do something active together outdoors. This could be a social occasion, e.g. a walk, or a 'make space' day in which you work together to make your outdoor area a more enjoyable place to be.

Emotional intelligence

Taking responsibility for our behaviour, omissions and mistakes is essential for resilience. Resilient teams develop a culture where it is OK to make mistakes and learn from them. Emotional intelligence requires emotional maturity and taking responsibility for our feelings as well as recognising and acknowledging the feelings of others. It involves understanding how emotions can affect our behaviour and the behaviour of others. Creating a space between stimulus and response is key to emotional maturity, self-regulation and wisdom. So, if someone says or does something which is hurtful or makes you angry, instead if firing back a response or showing how feel straight away, you can take a moment to think, 'what response is going to be most helpful in this situation? If I was advising a friend how to respond, what would I say to them?'. This is a moment where you are free to choose –

to be curious rather than furious. What prompted this action? What prompted my reaction? What response would create most the kindness for everyone involved including myself? The age-old advice of taking a deep breath or counting to ten is useful!

Lack of emotional intelligence and responsibility for behaviour within a team has a profound impact on the team's resilience and relationships. Without emotional intelligence, it is easy for a culture of blame to develop. There will be open displays of anger or hostility, or whispered moans, complaints or nasty criticism in corridors. This kind of emotional climate saps the energy and enthusiasm from a place and group. Individuals may well start to feel physically or mentally unwell as a result. They may feel unable to spring back or feel unsupported to face difficulties as they arise.

On reflection

EMOTIONAL INTELLIGENCE

Reflecting on our own emotional state and behaviours can be useful in order to understand what gets us into emotional hot water. What makes us anxious or behave in ways that we later regret? Cultivating that space between a 'stimulus' and a 'response' will help us contain, manage and use our feelings most effectively for ourselves AND those around us. We can ask:

- Am I aware of my habitual triggers and reactions?

- Do I take responsibility for my own feelings and reactions?

- How good am I at expressing difficult feelings appropriately?

- Do I have habits that help support positive emotional states or do people often respond negatively to me?

As a team, we can ask ourselves:

- How are we at taking responsibility for our feelings, behaviours and reactions?

- How well do we, as a team, allow difficult feelings to be appropriately expressed?

- How do we manage conflict?

- How do we avoid getting sucked into 'hidden' gossip, moans or gripes and bring concerns up in positive spirit of cooperation?

See the further reading section at the end of this chapter for practical resources to help.

Connection and support

Connection and support is not just about people. It is also about connection to place and how comfortable you feel where you live and work. However, it is often more about having someone to talk to who understands where you are coming from. Listening well and being listened to is a key aspect of resilience.

On reflection

CONNECTION AND SUPPORT

Taking time to reflect on and develop our sources of support is useful. Support needs to be thought about and cultivated – it does not just 'occur'. So ask yourself:

- Who do I go to talk about my wellbeing?
- Who do I go to talk about my work?

Create a 'circle of support'. Name all the people and places that support you. Think about who you would go to when you are in a predicament or have a dilemma at work. Who do you enjoy listening to?

As a team, you can think about:

- How can we deepen collaboration and support in our team?
- How do we give constructive feedback as a team for development and growth? Think about peer-to-peer coaching, good supervision practice and well-facilitated and prepared staff meetings.
- How connected are we to the natural world around us?
- How connected is our place of work with the neighbourhood?

Talk in your team or your family about your connection to the place you live and work. Reach out to others in your community, e.g. people who live and work locally. Ask them about what they love about the community.

On reflection

DISCERNMENT AND WISDOM

For yourself, think about how you learn best.

Ask yourself:

- Who are the wisest people you have met in your life?
- How have they behaved that has made you think of them as wise?

Questions for your team:

- How do we learn best together?
- What have our best moments of learning been this year?
- What do we tend to avoid that needs looking at?
- Who has helped us?
- Do we have a blame culture or is OK to own up to mistakes?
- What more can we do to learn from each other and create time to think?

Purpose and meaning

We need to feel that our work has purpose and that it is aligned with our values. If we feel we are being asked to do things we don't really believe in, it can make us feel put upon, undervalued and undermined – all of which leads to depletion in our resilience. If, however, we have work that is aligned with our values and we feel we are contributing usefully to the team and to the aims, outcomes and impact of the work, this feeds our resilience. When we worked with nature, the living environment and our care for it becomes a core purpose of our work.

PURPOSE AND MEANING

Consider the following questions individually and/or as a team:

- What are my core values and how do I live them out in my life?

- Can I think of a specific moment when I have held a boundary around my values at any time in my life?

- What is the purpose of this team and how does it fit within the purpose of the organisation as a whole? What is the value of my role within this purpose?

- How does this connect with my individual values?

- How does the environment feed or deplete my purpose?

- What do I say 'yes' to and what do I say 'no' to?

Resilient children – a systemic view

Throughout this book we have taken a systemic approach to looking at child development and working outdoors, recognising that we all live in and with many systems that we shape and that shape us as we grow older.

Spiritual system – being connected to something bigger than ourselves and our immediate experience in the body

Ecological system – interdependence, connection with the environment and the living planet

Social and political system – the influence of community and government (environment, food produvtion, economic wellbeing, education)

Family and cultural system – family cultural beliefs, values and customs

Felt systems – the sense windows of survival, wellbeing, independence and meaning, including the deep structures of language, expression and thought.

Body system – the way we perceive through our senses, our bodies and actions

The many systems that support child development

When looking at children's resilience, we can use the resilience wheel model shown below. The key ingredients of resilience map well onto holistic and process-orientated approaches to child development and learning.

Dicernment and wisdom
Children's sense of self, theory of mind

Self-care
Children's independence with self-care routines

Purpose and meaning
Children's agency and entrepreneurship

RESILIENCE

Vitality and flow
Children's wellbeing and engagement

Emotional intelligence
Emotional awareness, empathy and self-regulation

Connection and support
Attachment to key people and to place

Resilience and child development

Working with children outside and connecting them to nature provides an expanded arena in which children develop all aspects of resilience. Spending extended time outdoors and working with the natural elements around us gives us abundant additional resources to support children's resilience and our own.

In practice

RESILIENCE OUTDOORS

We can resource children's resilience with nature in so many ways. Here are a few suggestions:

VITALITY AND FLOW

- Give children nature-rich outdoor spaces in which to explore and roam.

- Try not to interrupt their concentration and engagement unnecessarily. Routines can sometimes be interrupted. A snack time or circle time can be delayed if some other activity, learning or conversation is in full flow.

- When appropriate, ask good questions and encourage children to move slightly out of their comfort zone, to try new things and to take some risks.

- Notice children's particular interests and encourage their 'genius'. Allow them to become completely involved and encourage investigations and skills practice.

SELF-CARE

- Feed children good food, teaching them how to grow it and prepare it for eating.

- Give them plenty of opportunities to be active and move, run, climb, roll, dance, crawl, hop and skip. How many different ways of walking can you discover?

- Give them space to relax and daydream amongst the beauty of nature. Babies often sleep particularly well outdoors.

Nature-rich spaces in which to explore and roam

CONNECTION AND SUPPORT

- Support children to develop relationships with other children outdoors through games and collective problem-solving activities.

- Encourage children to build relationships with and connect with the non-human world of plants, trees and animals as well as their peers and adults.

- Talking about feelings and difficulties can sometimes be easier outside than inside.

EMOTIONAL INTELLIGENCE

- Encourage children to talk about their feelings outdoors – what places and things, e.g. flowers, do they like or dislike? What things make them happy or sad? What scares them?

- Encourage children to bounce back after a scraped knee or getting wet feet and to know how to take care themselves. For example, show them how to dry themselves off after getting wet.

DISCERNMENT AND WISDOM

- Teach them to look for and understand the signs of nature, e.g. that spring is on its way or that there is a storm coming.

- Teach them the names of common plants and birds, their habits and properties, why they are important for us and how we can support them.

- Give them lots of opportunities to problem solve and find things out for themselves. Ask more open questions, e.g. why do you think nettles sting? What do you think happens to snails when the weather is dry? How might we build a bridge to cross that stream?

PURPOSE AND MEANING

- Give them apprenticeship tasks with outcomes that you value – sweeping up, building something, growing something, preparing a dish or a meal

- Help children to plant trees and take care of them, feed birds in the winter and create bug hotels and log piles for hibernating creatures.

Narrative

JENSEN: PLANTING TREES

Jensen wanted to help plant the tree. He was the most enthusiastic of the group and took the lead. He looked at the label and talked about what kind of tree it was. Most of all, he wanted to use the real spade to dig a hole. It took time and a bit of support from his teacher to learn the most efficient way to hold the spade and how to use his foot to get the spade to dig down, then how to lift the soil. He maintained focused attention and struggled but persevered through this initial difficulty. Every gesture showed purpose, confidence and determination. His questions about the tree and the label showed that the task had meaning. He was developing his sense of balance and orientation. He was learning about trees and what they need to grow as he went along. Later that year or next year, he will harvest and eat the fruit form the tree. He was developing his resilience and his knowledge of, and connection to, the wider ecological world.

Tree planting

The four Gs: gateways to nature, connection and resilience

The four Gs – gratitude, guidance, grit and glory – are dispositions that are developed with practise. They are gateways to developing a deep-level connection with nature. The four Gs are practices which come from 'deep ecology' where we see ourselves as part of the living Earth, and our wellbeing is connected to our sense of our place within it. The four Gs are grounded in the belief that we protect the things that we love, and if children learn to love the living world around them, they will also learn how to protect it. The four Gs have a spiritual dimension in that they are also grounded in the belief that we are connected to something bigger than ourselves as individuals. Many spiritual traditions will recognise these practices as not inconsistent with their own. However, they are not linked to any particular religion. Whether you consider yourself to be Humanist, Christian, Muslim, Jewish, Buddhist, Atheist or other, you should find that these dispositions to working with nature are compatible with other beliefs.

Gratitude

> 'Gratitude is liberating. It is subversive. It helps us to realize that we are sufficient, and that realization frees us.'
>
> Joanna Macy

Experience in nature can bring a sudden rush of gratitude and happiness. Focusing on what we are grateful for in our lives can shift our perspective from 'glass half empty' to 'glass half full'. Research confirms that having a sense of gratitude can improve our mental wellbeing, mood, happiness and productivity. It seems that gratitude is something that you can grow with practice; the more you practise being grateful, the stronger and more stable it becomes within you. Employees of successful and happy organisations say that gratitude and appreciation is one of the key reasons why they enjoy their place of work. Of course, gratitude and appreciation have to be genuine. Some people seem to have a more natural capacity for gratitude for others. But everyone can practise and develop it.

Showing gratitude and appreciation is something children will learn from their teachers and carers through modelling and coaching as part of your daily learning journeys together. Many cultures celebrate festivals dedicated to gratitude and thanksgiving – often focused on harvest time. Working in nature, we have many opportunities to notice and be grateful – for the sun that warms us; for rain that brings us water; for the air that we breathe; for the food we eat; for the animals that providers with wool, leather, eggs, meat; for the plants that provide us cotton, hemp; and the trees that provide us with shade, fruit, nuts, paper, furniture.

MINDFULNESS AND GRATITUDE PRACTICE

Mindfulness has many gratitude practices that you can learn by attending a course or from other mindfulness practitioners. Here are a few suggestions for gratitude practices that you can include in your routine:

'Five gratitudes' practice

Think of five things you are grateful for each evening before you go to sleep. This might simply be things about your body, e.g. 'I am grateful for my breath, my life, for my two hands and feet, my comfortable bed and the roof over my head'. It might be things that have happened in the day, e.g. 'I am grateful that I have a bed and roof over my head. I am grateful for the breakfast I enjoyed this morning. I am grateful for the friend I drank coffee with today. I am grateful that I can afford to go out for coffee. I am grateful for the companionship of my cat'.

As you get the hang of it, you can start to think about what you are grateful for at different times of day.

'Time for gratitude' practice

Choose specific times in which to practise gratitude every day. Say a silent 'thank you' the first time you look out of the window each day, or every time you brush your teeth, or every time you walk in through the gate of your workplace.

Gratitude journal

Some people keep a gratitude journal by their bed or on their mobile phone to list the new things they are grateful for each day.

Gratitude smiles

Smile as you think about what you are grateful for. It has been scientifically proven that the very act of smiling – stretching the muscles on your face – makes your brain release more happiness hormones!

GRATITUDE OUTDOORS

Children are good at gratitude practice if you give them the opportunities to practise and you encourage it. When you go outdoors each day, ask the children 'What can we be thankful for today?' Once you have drawn their attention to some things, they will quickly find more. You might start with:

The weather

- For the sun that warms us.

- For the rain that gives us water and make the trees green.

Keeping us warm and dry

- For our welly boots that mean we can jump in puddles without getting wet.

- To our mums, dads, grannies, carers for buying our clothes and remembering to bring them in when it rains.

- For the gardener or caretaker and the jobs they do to keep us safe and for looking after the environment.

The living world around such birds, minibeasts and worms

- For singing their songs.

- For clearing the ground of leaves, compost, rotten wood.

For trees and plants

- For giving us shade.

- For making delicious scents.

- For making the air fresh to breathe.

When picking fruit or vegetables, you can encourage children to say 'thank you' to the plant as they pick.

THANKS AND APPRECIATION WALL

Another nice way to encourage gratitude is to create an indoor or outdoor space where people can write or mark their thanks for particular acts of kindness or goodwill. If outside, make it somewhere beautiful – with hanging baskets or wall-mounted plants. It can be in a place that parents and children see when they arrive. Laminate thank you cards or pictures to hang between baskets or planters.

Narrative

THE CEDARSONG FOREST KINDERGARTEN

Children at the Cedarsong school near Seattle, USA, are taught about which plants are edible from early on in their Early Years education. They are even taught how to pick nettles and to eat the fresh shoots without getting stung. If they are using nature's materials for art or play, they are taught only to use what has fallen to the ground – dead wood, petals, stones, etc. If they pick food to eat, they are taught to say thank you to the plant as they pick. The founder of Cedarsong and teacher trainer Erin Kenny calls this 'compassion scaffolding'. Children spend the whole session outdoors. They are taught that their nursery is a sanctuary for *all* living things and to express gratitude every day.

Guidance

There are lots of ways to learn about nature. We can learn about nature through the scientific study of rocks, plants, animals. We can learn *in* nature which we call outdoor learning. We can also learn *through* nature experience, and we can learn from and with nature. When we learn through and from nature experience, we can allow our analytical mind some respite while we move into other ways of sensing using creativity, imagination and intuition.

Children can be supported to experience nature's elements when working with nature's materials in art and craft projects. Getting to understand the properties and gifts that these materials bring comes from direct experience with them. We can also use movement to unlock our unconscious memory and make creative connections. Many philosophers and scientists have had their 'eureka' moments while walking or sitting in nature. Taking time out in nature can refresh and renew our thinking, giving us inspiration or allowing a knotty or complex problem to unravel.

Learning from nature

On reflection

ASK A QUESTION – SEE WHAT YOU GET

Here is a fun exercise to get you outdoors. It may surprise you!

Next time you go out for a walk, try thinking of a question you have that you need an answer for. It could be how to handle a particular conversation or relationship or how to organise an event, for example. Hold it lightly in your mind and make sure the questions you have are clear. Then go for a walk and see what you are drawn to, e.g. a place to sit or something to stop and stare at. Every time you stop, ask the question to the nearest tree or the river, a cloud or a flower – whatever aspect of nature you are drawn to. Then tune your attention to 'listening' to the answer from the object of your attention. Do this three or four times. When you have finished your walk, spend a few moments reflecting on your experience. Are you any clearer about the answer to your question?

Since ancient times, nature has inspired storytellers to use its metaphors to pass on teaching, guidance and wisdom. Just think about the stories you already know and love and how many of them are about plants, animals, trees, journeys, rivers, sea, mountains and flowers – from traditional tales to ancient myths.

Tribal people with a long tradition of storytelling have passed on stories and myths about how things are made, how the animals came to be and how people lived and travelled the land in the past. Stories were how we communicated from tribe to tribe – a way we kept our history and traditions alive – long before the invention of ink and paper or print, film or media. Storytelling is how we survived.

Storytelling is still a way in which we share, imagine and celebrate the things we value – even though the medium of stories has changes and continued to change. It is often a particularly important means by which we can bridge gaps between differences in lifestyles and beliefs, and where pride and dignity in our culture can flourish.

Tales from nature have been told across the world since language began. They have been passed down in storytelling, as well as, paintings, writing, film and other media. In the last few decades, the film industry has produced many stories which use nature as their inspiration, and these are incredibly popular with young children.

A sense of place

In practice

NATURE AS TEACHER THROUGH STORIES

Take storytelling outside! Create a storytelling space in your outside area if you can. In winter, this might be around a fire (a traditional place for telling tales).

- Encourage children and their parents or carers to share their favourite nature story.

- Make a collection of traditional nature tales.

- Children's imaginations easily pick up the idea of stories from nature; ask them if they can find a story from a tree or a flower using these prompts:

  - 'If that tree could talk what do you think it would say?'

  - 'Put your ear against the tree – can you hear the tree's secrets?'

  - 'Lie on the ground and look at the clouds. What do you think they are saying to each other?'

  - 'Listen to the bird song. What do you think the bird is singing about in bird language?'

Make books about the stories inspired by your garden – or from your adventures beyond.

Stories in nature and stories about nature help children to understand themselves and the world

Grit

Nature is not always or only about beauty and inspiration. In nature, we can see every day reminders that life is not permanent. Seasons come and go, trees and plants flourish, die and then sprout new leaves again. We find dead birds or insects on our path. We know that nature contains that can harm us; stories of hurricanes and floods and other natural disasters feature regularly on our screens. Resilience is about developing the capacity to weather the storms, feel grief and anger and develop knowledge of death without becoming completely overwhelmed by it. Facing adversity is necessary and resilience gives us the physical, emotional and mental capacities to 'bounce back' and to stay present and connected to our daily life. Mindfulness offers us great tools for this. Sometimes a tough challenge can transform us for the better – give us strength, develop our sense of humility and our sense of humour. Like the grain of sand in an oyster, sometimes the grit of life creates pearls of wisdom and grace.

Narrative

POLLY: THE GRIT OF LIFE IN EARLY YEARS

At 16 months, Polly was already a real nature explorer – she loved grass, flowers and animals. She touched everything. The world of nature was there to please her, and she was clearly pleased by it.

One day, when her carers were not watching, she got stung by a nettle. She screamed with pain and confusion. Her language was not developed enough to allow her to explain her pain and fury, so she bit her carer's arm to show her what she was feeling. Her carer's response was gentle but not overly dramatic. Polly's relationship with nature will never be quite as innocent as before. She learned that some plants can hurt her. When she was two, she learned the same thing about wasps – not all insects are harmless. When she was three, the pet goldfish was found dead swimming the bowl. Another surprise! What does dead mean? Why do we bury it?

At each stage, the carer's role was to be sympathetic but also matter of fact. These things happen. She explained in the best way possible about stings and why they happen, how to avoid them and how to treat them. She allowed the death of the goldfish to be a learning experience for the whole group – giving the children a lot of time to notice and talk about what was different about the goldfish now that it was dead and allow them to ask questions. In some cases, they referred to a death they already knew about – most commonly a pet or grandparent. This was a good time to put a name to difficult feelings.

A sense of place

Narrative

MATTHEW: THE TREE BLOOD STORY

Some favourite trees in the woodland used by our nursery had to be severely pollarded as they were crack willows and had grown too tall, presenting a danger to the children. At first it was shocking for the children to see their tree friend cut down, but as the logs had been left, they became a place for climbing and adventure, finding new creatures and developing a new landscape for learning. A discovery of pooled sap and water in the crook of one tree was identified by one of the children as 'tree blood' which led to multiple stories and investigations into whether tree sap was like blood, what blood was for and when the children had seen their own blood. It was also an opportunity to tell the story of the tree and how healthy new growth was starting to sprout from the pollarded trunks in the ground.

Discovering the 'tree blood'

In practice

LOSS AND DIFFICULT TRANSITIONS

There are many ways of encouraging children to talk about their feelings if they have experienced loss or difficult transitions.

WORRY TREE

Choose a tree or sturdy plant to become your 'worry tree'. Tell a story about it and how its purpose is to listen to the things we are worried about. You can write what the children say on paper leaves and tie them to the tree – where the wind will listen to them and blow away their worries.

Reassurance from friends in nature

WISHING WELL

Underneath a wishing tree, you might want to create a 'wishing well'. This can be a deep bowl of water surrounded by nice stones and moss, for example. Have another bowl of small pebbles or glass beads. The children can choose a small pebble to drop into the 'well' when they name something they are hoping will change or get better.

MEMORY GARDEN

Making a memory garden can be a good way to help children talk about their feelings of loss. The death of a nursery pet or finding a dead bird might be an occasion to find a place to bury its body in the garden and plan a plant in its memory. You could make a little plaque – laminated pictures drawn by a child or several children – in appreciation of the positive things that the pet contributed to your lives before it died. Let the children's responses to the idea be your guide as to who should be involved and how much attention to give it.

MOVING ON PLANT

When children are moving on from your setting – to start school perhaps – you can plant seeds some weeks before and use their growth as a metaphor to help them grow strong enough to be moved to a new place. The children can then take the shoots home when they leave as a living memory of their time in your setting.

Glory

> 'Those who contemplate the beauty of the earth find reserves of strength that will endure as long as life lasts. There is something infinitely healing in the repeated refrains of nature — the assurance that dawn comes after night, and spring after winter.'
>
> Rachel Carson, Silent Spring

Awe is that sense of wonder we feel in the presence of something vast that expands and maybe transcends our understanding of the world and our place within it. This feeling is perhaps best captured by poets or in the descriptions of peak experiences from explorers such as mountain climbers. We will all have experienced awe at some point in our lives at the sight of a beautiful sunset, for example, or a piece of art, a religious experience or a piece of music.

Young children are open and alive to awe and wonder, if they are given space and time to stop and stare. Everything is new and fresh to them. As teachers and carers, working with young children in nature gives us many opportunities to reawaken our own sense of wonder.

Time to stop and stare – daydreaming is important

Narrative

BILLY: WOW MOMENTS

Billy, aged two and half, ran ahead of the group through the wood. It was winter and got dark soon after 4 p.m. We had gone into the woods at about 2:30 p.m. and, as the woods were already very dense and shaded, we had not noticed the gradual fading of the light. It was now getting on for 4 p.m. and time to go back. As Billy ran out of the woods, he stopped in amazement. The sky was lit red and orange with an amazing sunset sky. He threw himself on his back and pointed shouting 'Sky! Sky!'. Despite the cold, we all lay down with him to wonder with awe at the glory of the sky.

Narrative

MAIA: 'RENBO!'

Coming over the hill on a mixed weather day, we saw a beautiful double rainbow ahead. We stopped, and the teacher pointed: 'Wow! A rainbow!'. Maia, aged 18 months, looked agape. Suddenly she pointed too. 'Wow! Renbo! Wow! Renbo!' she called excitedly out loud as she ran full tilt towards it.

A sense of place

Research has shown what we probably already know ourselves, that experiences of awe and wonder can foster humility, kindness and altruism as well as other pro-social behaviours. Young children's sense of awe is wide open because so many of their experiences are new and their sense doorways to the world are wide open. Seeing the moon or the sea for the first time, or even the movement of a snail across the floor may delight and grip our children in a way we can only imagine. The Earth and our bodies work together and there is wonder in the beauty around us that we can notice every day – the opening of a new flower, a blackbird in full throttle, the pattern of a snail shell, the way an anthill is organised, the appearance of a rainbow. Our planet Earth is incredible.

In practice

AWE AND WONDER OUTDOORS

As teachers, we can pay attention to these moments, giving children the time to pause, breathe in the experience, and then delight or exclaim. We can allow daydreaming, with opportunities to slow down, lie down, or to stop and stare. We can attune to the children's experience – following their breath and their smallest movements. Often awe experiences act on a deep level and need time to sink in. They might be beyond everyday words and these experiences can be ruined by adults jumping in with questions or explanations. We can be alert and spontaneous. Don't over plan.

A nature-rich environment will provide awe and wonder experiences without needing to try to make them happen. Make your outside area a place where children can experience some of the following:

*   The opening of a new flower.

*   The sound of a blackbird or thrush singing in spring.

*   The flight of a butterfly.

*   The hatching of a chick or the development of a tadpole.

*   Creatures of all kinds under fallen logs and stones.

*   Insects visiting wild flowers and plants.

What have been your children's awe and wonder moments so far? Depending on where you live and the season, go and visit places nearby where children can see:

*   The tallest tree around.

*   Wild water, e.g. streams, rivers, waterfalls or the sea).

*   An expanse of freshly fallen snow.

*   A wide expanse of sky.

*   The moon and stars on a winter evening.

*   A herd of sheep or cattle (especially if there are baby lambs or calves around).

*   A murmuring of starlings or flocks of geese and ducks.

Resilience in your setting

Your place of work and care for children is a system in itself, whether you are in a nursery, preschool or family home. A system is a set of relationships that work together to function as a whole. Your body is a system with organs, blood and the exchange of fluids and nutrients. A garden pond or a piece of woodland are systems as both have interdependent elements such as soil, plants, creatures which exchange nutrients, water and gases. Your family is a system – the exchange of relationships support other parts of the system. For a system to be healthy and resilient, it needs to be nurtured, just like a garden. The next exercise will help you identify what needs attention right now.

Further reading

To find out more about the ideas in this chapter, search online for:

❀ Doctor Chatterjee's book, *The 4 Pillars of Health*

❀ Erin Kenny and Forest Kindergarten's book, *The Cedarsong Way*

❀ 'The resilience wheel' by Routes to Resilience.

On reflection

RESILIENCE IN YOUR WORK SETTING

First, draw a picture of your work setting as a garden. (If you don't like drawing, you can use clay or found objects from nature to represent the elements of your system.) Imagine that you are the gardener. What are you trying to grow? You might draw flowers or vegetables to represent the healthy happy children.

Then ask yourself these questions and add more to your drawing/map as you go along to represent how you will support resilience:

- What's flourishing? (Are some children doing better than others? Are some team members doing better than others?)

- What seeds do you want to sow? (What new ideas do you have for the coming year? How many new children, staff or volunteers do you want to attract?)

- Which plants need nurture, water or shelter? (Which children, relationships, parents, resources or environment that need your attention?)

- What needs cutting back or pruning? (Is there too much of some kinds of behaviour or is there paperwork that is getting in the way of enabling you to flourish?)

- Are there any pests that need attention – those things that buzz around in your brain or eat up your attention unnecessarily?

- What is the fertiliser? (What gives you energy and joy for learning?)

- Who are the pollinators? How do you get ideas and inspiration? Is there any training or reading you want to do or other team members want to do? Do you have a mentor or critical friend who helps you develop?

This is a great team exercise to help people talk about what is needed to keep the whole system flourishing.

A sense of place

Nature pedagogy, community and conscious action

'The least movement is of importance to all nature. The entire ocean is affected by a pebble.'

Blaise Pascal

Chapter overview

This book brings together many ideas about working with young children outdoors and working with nature as our primary resource for wellbeing, resilience and learning. Our job is to give children the best start in life we can. We also have a responsibility to tend the wider system in which these early experiences happen and to look after the natural resources that are both their heritage and inheritance. We are stewards for places in which children can thrive in the present and from which they can also look to the future with confidence. We can do this by paying attention to the immediate environment of the places we live and work. We can work with our children to learn to understand the impact of our actions on others and the wider living world. We can engage with our wider community to stand up for what we believe will help create a better world. We can develop education systems where eco-literacy is valued as much as any other literacy in the curriculum.

Key ideas

- Environment matters – tending the garden
- Nature is our only true investment fund – education for sustainability
- A pedagogy for nature
- Source to resource
- Think global, act local
- Conscious community action

Environment matters – tending the garden

'It has been said that the environment should act as a kind of aquarium which reflects the ideas, ethics, attitudes and cultures of the people who live in it. This is what we are working toward.'

Loris Malaguzzi

Wherever we work with children, we work within a wider system of relationships, time and the environment. These things provide a container or a garden in which children grow and learn. Like gardeners with tender new plants, as teachers and carers we nourish and protect. Like gardeners, we need to work with the conditions of soil and climate, we need good tools and patience, skill and experience. A good gardener learns how to strengthen the fertility and nutrients of the soil with good compost and to flex what they do with different plants at different times. Similarly, good teachers and carers learn how to provide a rich learning environment in which children can flourish through their experiences and by learning from others. We learn when to protect children and when they need to be slowly exposed to the elements in order to develop their resilience.

Education for sustainability

Our children will be left with the legacy of the environment we create. They are the scientists, engineers and philosophers of the future who will need to find solutions to the challenges that we have created. It is our responsibility to help them equip themselves with the tools and understanding and skills with which to do this. It is in their Early Years that children develop the disposition for enquiry and investigation – the early research skills that will assist them throughout life.

Our lives depend on the resources of nature: water, air and food. The things we eat come from nature, but often have been so processed that we don't recognise their natural source. A lot of our clothes and material products are made from synthetic fibres that are produced from carbon materials, such as coal and oil, or obtained from plant extraction, such as castor oil, soya and hemp. Money is only useful as a means of exchange. Ultimately, everything we use money for comes from nature at its source. We can have no economy without ecology. Human overconsumption, greed and competition can ultimately undermine the source of our survival. That is what sustainability is about – understanding that there needs to be a fine balance of what we put in and what we take out of our environment. Scientist are using the benefits of technology to find ways to use sources of energy that are in abundance – wind, sun and tidal power. It will take artists, engineers, investors, philosophers, communicators, people with imagination and skill to find ways of managing the impact of our waste materials – particularly plastics which do not degrade, and to bring the human population into balance with rest of the living world that sustains it.

Children develop their disposition of enquiry in the Early Years

On reflection

THINKING ABOUT OUR EDUCATION FOR SUSTAINABILITY

Look around at everyday things used in your work – materials, toys, first aid kit, toothbrush, furniture, etc. Choose a couple of items to explore by yourself or with your team. Pick useful things that you would not want to do without. Think about where each item came from.

- How did it become the object or material it is now?

- How many people were involved in the process of getting all the ingredients from the Earth, manufacturing it, packaging it and getting it to where it is now?

- What would happen if the world ran out of the source materials for this product?

- Could you do without this product?

- Could you use something else that used less energy – or was created using less energy or producing less waste?

As a starting point for developing your framework for sustainability, you could think about:

- How can we reduce use of plastics in our work environment?

- How can we move towards using more whole and less processed food?

- How can we reduce the waste we produce and find out what happens to it after we put it in the bin?

A sense of place

What kind of education is needed for our times? Education is at the centre of political debates; it is seen as the essential vehicle for influencing the minds of a future generation of leaders, voters, workers and the key to nations' economic success. In tribal cultures and in places where children grow up with a closer connection to the land and the outdoors, learning is more intimately connected with the stuff of life – with plants, animals and the elements of water, fire, rock, stone, snow. Learning *about* nature is learning *with* nature. Survival is dependent on the everyday sense experiences of wet, warm, cold, hungry, fed, safe, alert, looking, hearing, smelling, tasting, dark and light. In hunter gatherer and early agrarian peasant communities, children grew up in and around everything that fed and sheltered them. They learned through close observation of the life-cycles of plants and animals. In post-industrial societies, we have become disconnected from nature as the source of our survival. Indeed, we create and consume more and more products that pollute our waters (non-biodegradable plastic waste), the lands (chemicals and non-biodegradable waste) and our air (burning fossil fuels for energy).

Children from hunter-gatherer and early agrarian cultures learned skills as apprentices to their carers – accompanying them in their work and joining in with tasks that ensured the survival of the tribe or the village as soon as they were able. In our post-industrial culture, children are freed from the demands of working for their survival, and instead they spend long years in classrooms, learning from the simulated and imaginary worlds contained in books and screens that have been created for them by others.

Measuring what is important

Children's development has been studied, analysed and dissected into small parts and developmental milestones. The drive for accountability and progress means that we restrict teaching to things we can measure and test. For example, our understanding of language and literacy education has focused on decoding phonics, rather than the living, lively, versatile ways in which we share our thoughts and receive communication from others. We have less trust in the professional judgement of teachers and carers. We have moved towards a centralised curriculum framework, a model of child development that focuses on testing what can be measured and a system where relationships and the learning environment is governed by the stringent regulation and paperwork of health and safety, child protection and preventing discomfort.

Nettle burgers

In practice

THE HERITAGE OF COMMON PLANTS

The use of plants for human benefit has evolved over hundreds of years. Plant products are everywhere you look, e.g. dyes for clothing, perfumes, soaps and medicines. Children will enjoy learning about the properties of plants from a very early age. Choose three plants that grow abundantly near you, e.g. nettle, elder and mint. You can grow all these in your garden or find them in other people's gardens (ask before taking any!). Here are some ideas for using them:

NETTLE

- Make tea by boiling a few nettle leaves in water. This is rich in iron.

- Make nettle burgers by combining cooked nettles and oats with flavourings of your choice.

- Use nettles to dye some fabric – or even eggs! You need to make a high concentration of dye by boiling lots of nettles and allowing them to steep. (Onion skins are another very satisfying plant dye material.)

MINT

- Make tea by boiling a few leaves in water. This is good for digestion.

- Make 'toothpaste' by boiling peppermint leaves and mixing the water with bicarbonate of soda and little grapeseed oil.

ELDERFLOWER

- Make elderflower cordial in spring (you will find many recipes on the Internet) or fry the flowers in batter – delicious!

- Make elderberry dye with berries.

- Use the stems of the elderflower for making homemade pencils. Simply cut pencil length sticks, hollow out the soft centre with a skewer and replace with a charcoal stick. Children could then decorate the pencils to personalise them.

Our consumerist culture equates happiness with creating comfortable lives at all cost, protecting and insuring ourselves from risk. This culture encourages us to avoid facing the fact that we all have a limited lifespan on Earth. It distracts us with entertainment, activity and the need for material 'stuff'. We lose our sense of interdependence with our environment and our awareness that what we do now will affect generations to come. This includes our children's or their children's capacity to feed themselves, survive and thrive.

Perhaps it is high time for a rethink. We can't and would not want to put the clock back. Life for children in hunter-gatherer and early agrarian societies was by no means idyllic. We have the huge gifts of better medicine, more comfort, expanded communication, greater diversity and richness – all of which benefit human kind and are not in themselves necessarily harmful to the planet. But we may also have lost sight of something along the way. As teachers and carers, we can contribute to a wider discussion about the fundamental purposes of education and how it best serves children and their future on this planet.

Children develop their disposition of enquiry in the Early Years

A pedagogy for nature

'If a child is to keep alive his inborn sense of wonder, he needs the companionship of at least one adult who can share it, rediscovering with him the joy, excitement, and mystery of the world we live in.'

Rachel Carson

Ecological identity

Through spending extended time outdoors tuning in to what is happening in nature, children can see plants, rocks and animals as intimately related to their life and their survival. When they marvel at the beauty in nature and retain a sense wonder and love for other life forms, they grow up wanting to protect it. When we gain a sense of our place in the wider scheme of things, we develop and embrace elements of our ecological identity. We feel a deep attachment to the Earth. We feel at home in the world and are rooted like trees. We have the confidence of knowing we belong here – no matter how far we travel.

We can see and measure children's ecological identities as they are expressed through signs of their wellbeing and engagement when they are outside in nature. We see it in the relationships they form – not just with other children and adults but also with special places, animals, with found objects and the landscape of their community.

Ecological literacy

Ecological literacy is scientific, mathematical, imaginative and spiritual learning which comes from a direct experience of nature and developing understanding of how things work and fit together. We become more 'eco-literate' through learning about the names of things in nature, discovering their properties and how they can be used. We can develop our eco-literacy by learning the languages in nature, exploring different habits, and holding a deep understanding that everything in nature affects everything else, including ourselves as human beings. We are made of the same stuff as stars and stones, plants and rain.

In practice

THE MANY GIFTS OF TREES

Getting to know trees in your area and the kind of wood that comes from them makes a wonderful ongoing investigation. Get to know your local forester or park service. Ask them to let you know when a tree is being cut down. Ask if the children can watch and if you can have some logs from the tree for your garden.

Here are some other wood-related activities for you to try in your setting:

- Encourage children to look around and make a collection of wooden things in your setting.

- If you know a musician who plays a wooden musical instrument such as a violin, cello or oboe, ask them to come and play.

- Look for a green wood worker who can demonstrate whittling a wooden spoon or making a stool from wood.

- Talk to your local woodland or wildlife trust about how you and your children can get involved in planting trees.

- Make your own charcoal in a small biscuit tin.

YOU WILL NEED:

- ✦ an old metal biscuit tin or similar
- ✦ wood sticks – enough to pack the tin (willow or hazel work well)
- ✦ a tool to pierce a hole in the lid, e.g. a screwdriver
- ✦ heat-proof fire gloves;
- ✦ a small fire in your fire pit or fire bowl.

1. Pack the tin tightly with cut willow.

2. Pierce a hole in the lid (important!). It is good if the lid is also loose fitting.

3. Place the tin on the fire and keep watching it. Smoke will come out of the hole and underneath the lid. It is highly flammable and will catch fire. Watch it carefully. Once the smoke stops coming out of the hole, your charcoal is done.

4. Take it out of the fire carefully and leave to cool. Then enjoy it!

Narrative

THE ONEOAK PROJECT

The OneOak project involved children in harvesting acorns from a 222-year-old oak tree to plant a new forest once the oak tree was felled. The children watched the tree being cut down and followed the story of the wood. A travelling exhibition was created of the great many products that the tree gifted to humans: beautiful hand-carved furniture and a commemorative bench, firewood, charcoal, a ceiling truss for a timber-framed building, paper and many art projects. The children planted a new oak forest from the acorns. They learned about how trees enhance our lives in many ways. They learned about the lifecycle of trees and how they could help grow more trees for generations to come.

Well-known conservationists, environmentalists and scientists often describe how their fascination for and love of nature was gained through playing outside for hours in a 'free-range' childhood that let them explore and ponder the secrets of nature. If we want to raise children who will find solutions to the social and environmental challenges of the world today, they will need eco-literacy skills alongside the mainstream literacy and numeracy agenda. In their earliest years, this means learning about the environment through intimate sensory connection to nature's materials and diversity: walking barefoot on grass, stone and sand, modelling with mud, listening to birdsong, splashing in water, and getting to know the diversity of trees, plants and minibeasts in their neighbourhood. In doing these activities, children are laying the framework for understanding the living world.

However, spending lots of time outdoors may not in itself be enough to instil love for nature and a sense of connection, or the skills and understanding needed to protect it. As teachers and carers, we need to become mentors and companions and provide the landscapes and opportunities for an ecological identity to take root and ecological literacy to develop.

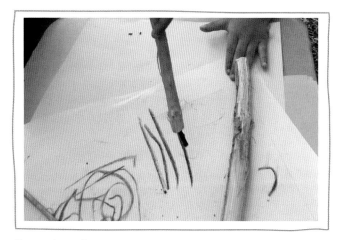

Charcoal pencils

From source to resource

Because many of us live in a world that is quite disconnected from nature as the source of the things we need every day, it is important to show children the connections. This chapter has several 'in practice' ideas for how we can do that. Children can learn early about the 'gifts' that nature offers us. Be prepared to answer ethical questions such as 'does it hurt a tree to be cut down?' If you eat meat, the animals that are the source of this nutrient will inevitably come up. There will be different cultural responses to these questions and sensitivity is needed to be non-judgmental of the beliefs and values of each child's home, their family's lifestyle choices or faith.

Meeting cows helps us understand where milk comes from

In practice

SOURCE TO RESOURCE

Food – from farm to plate

Growing and harvesting food shows children the journey of their food from farm to plate: from the tilling of the soil to the tasting of the meal. You might also keep chickens for eggs or visit somewhere you can see a cow or a goat being milked. It is great fun to put cream in a glass jar with a lid and get children to take turns shaking it until it turns to butter! Visit local beehives or get a beekeeper to visit and show you how honey extraction works. Pick blackberries and apples and make crumble. Do you have a local community orchard or somewhere with an apple juicer?

Wool – from sheep to shawl

Working with raw sheep's wool is a fantastic way to connect with nature. Very young children will enjoy seeing how wool is sheared from the sheep. They can get involved in washing and carding the wool. Depending on their age, they might also get involved in dying, weaving, felting and even knitting – or they might just enjoy watching others. Working with sheep's wool in this way is a is a wonderful opportunity to connect to the gifts that animals bring with the end product we wear.

If you work somewhere where it is possible for you to visit live cattle or sheep, take the children to meet them. Many farms are open to visitors during lambing season and some will bring an orphan bottle-fed lamb to your setting to meet the children. You might also have a local spinners and weavers' association who can help.

Grain – from field to bread

Gather some ripe wheat stalks in late summer. Use a hand-turned grain mill (a coffee mill will do) to grind the grains into flour. Make the flour into bread dough. Roll the dough into 'sausage' strips and wrap them around a stick. Cook the breadsticks over an open fire.

Think global, act local

There are excellent resources and ideas available that can help support you to implement a holistic environment policy, including activities young children and their parents can get involved in. The Permaculture Society, Eco-schools, Learning Through Landscapes and others have specifically designed audit tools, activity ideas and a wealth of knowledge for you to draw on. These cover:

Energy: Do you have any solar power in your setting? You can now get mini solar-powered toys and water pumps that are great for observing the impact of the sun.

Waste: Do you recycle? Do you have compost heap? How do you use it?

Chemicals: How do you decide what products to use (including cleaning products)? How do you assess their impact on the environment?

Water harvest: Do you have guttering on sloping roofs that produce a rainwater harvest? These are a great way for children to observe directly how rainwater accumulates and depletes in times of drought. Harvested rainwater is much better for plants than tap water.

It is great if you can use the expertise of people living and working in your community to get involved in your activities. Of course, many parents are at work and have limited opportunities to get involved with early education and childcare. However, using the environment as your focus for action can create opportunities for people to get involved according to their skills and interest. Everybody will have different ways they can comfortably engage with Earth-minded education.

The Children and Nature Network suggests four ways or 'spheres' in which people can choose to take action to make a difference:

✿ Personal (home)

✿ Community (neighbourhood)

✿ Institutional (team/nursery)

✿ Policy and education (local government, campaign groups).

The table below suggests what kind of action you might choose to take in each sphere. You might choose to only engage in one sphere – or in several, alone or with others, with your team or with children, parents and the community. Please add your own ideas too!

LEVEL OF ENGAGEMENT	POSSIBLE ACTIVITIES FOR STAFF

Personal	• Attend a course or workshop to increase skills.
	• Lead an area of curriculum development or accreditation through an environment programme such as eco-schools.
	• Encourage parents to:
	  ✦ Volunteer to lead an activity trip or outing outdoors
	  ✦ Share skills – gardening, craft, cooking, solar power
	  ✦ Raise funds for a project.

Community	• Invite people with local knowledge of environmental issues or who work outdoors as park keepers, coast guards, stewards or volunteers into the setting to meet the children. • Go on lots of local walks and journeys: visit local allotments, greenspaces, woods, trees, water sources, beaches, rivers. • Meet with local environmental organisations such as wildlife trusts. • Promote events put on other by other schools, settings or organisations in your area. • Put on community events – picnics, forest school sessions, nature explorer days (they can be fundraisers too!). • Look for unused spaces in the community and work together to develop them into community gardens, allotments, pocket parks, meeting places, safe spaces to play.
Institutions	• Become members of environmental support organisations for schools and Early Years (see end of this chapter for suggestions). • Develop an environmental policy (possibly as part of eco-schools accreditation) that looks at all aspects of your work and how it impacts on the environment. Explore national and international curriculum models for ideas to incorporate into your offer (see end of this chapter). • Make sure your routines allow children to be outside as much as possible. • Make sure all staff are comfortable with teaching and learning outdoors (it can be a requirement within a person and job specifications!). • Ensure everyone has the right clothing and skills to learn outdoors.
Policy and education	• Find out your local government and national government policies for the environment. • Lobby your local councillors and MPs for more focus on environmental education within education policy. • Join a national or global environmental campaigning organisation (see suggestions at end for further reading this chapter).

Conscious community action

The well-known African proverb says, 'it takes a village to raise a child'. In world of cities and towns, it is easy to lose our connections to extended family, friends and local support. An Early Years' setting such as a nursery or children's centre can be a hub for bringing people together by offering support, connection and possibilities for collective action.

Engaging parents and carers as the first educators of their children is essential. What happens at home is the most important influence on a child. Bringing parents together, giving them confidence and helping them build a sense of place with their children will bring huge benefits.

Festivals frequently involve food

FAMILIES, FESTIVALS AND FOOD

Celebrations, festivals and food are good ways to bring people from different cultures together outdoors. Harvest festivals of thanksgiving are celebrated by all faiths and cultures. These are times of connecting with nature through gratitude. If you are lucky enough to have families in your community celebrating these festivals, it can be a wonderful opportunity to ask them to bring food or show you how to prepare food, accompanied by traditional music, songs or customs. What better place to celebrate harvest than outdoors – where you can experience nature all around you?

Here are just some of the festivals that may be celebrated by your families:

- Sukkot (Feast of Booths or Tabernacles) is one of the three biblically-based pilgrimage holidays known as the shalosh regalim. It is an agricultural festival that originally was considered a thanksgiving for the fruit harvest.

- For Muslims, both the festivals of Eid al-Fitr and Eid al-Adha are occasions for showing gratitude to Allah and remembering Him, as well as giving alms to the poor.

- One of the very common practices of many indigenous American Indian or Canadian First Nation culture is some form of 'giveaway' as part of celebrations or rites of passage. Through a giveaway, you express your gratitude through sharing and giving away the gifts of nature you have accumulated – food, clothes, money – whatever you have.

- The Hindu festival of Pongal is directly associated with the annual cycle of seasons. It not only marks the reaping of the harvest, but also the withdrawal of the southeast monsoons in southern India.

A sense of place

Narrative

BARRACKS LANE COMMUNITY GARDEN – LOCAL ACTION FOR COMMUNITY AND WELLBEING

Barracks Lane garage site was a sad place. 28 asbestos-fabricated garages in the heart of Oxford had been abandoned and unused for many years. The site was filled with rubbish and burnt out cars. The land was toxic but used as an improvised playground by older children experimenting with drugs and as a storage zone for stolen goods. Occasionally the broken garages were used by homeless people to sleep and sadly one man died on the site. Oxford City Council invited suggestions as to what to do with that site. A group of local people took up the challenge, set up a charity, raised money to clear the site and create a community garden. 12 years later, the garden is blooming and much loved by the many groups and individuals who use it locally. It is simply a space – toxic wasteland turned into an oasis of wellbeing – a friendly and accessible place where everyone feels safe and at home. You can find out more about the project here: www.barrackslanegarden.org.uk.

As teachers and carers, we give young children lots of immersive experiences in nature. In urban areas, this may be through a small patch of earth and sky, through noticing the cracks in the pavement and the dandelions or other weeds that grow so resiliently even in areas of paving and concrete. We can take children on journeys – on trips or trails around the neighbourhood, seeking out pocket patches of park or places where food grows. We can make ethical choices in the materials we use and what we consume. We can walk our talk and live our values to demonstrate to others what we care about. We can draw on the natural and human resources of our community and neighbourhood. If we are open and inclusive, we can infect others with our enthusiasm to care for and be hopeful about our children's future on this beautiful planet.

> 'Never doubt that a small group of thoughtful, committed citizens can change the world; indeed, it's the only thing that ever has.'
>
> Margaret Mead

Further reading

To find out more about the ideas in this chapter, search online for:

- The Foundation for Environmental Education (http://www.fee.global)
- The Eco-Schools programme for Early Years (https://www.eco-schools.org.uk/)
- Liverpool John Moores University's specific resources for Early Years (https://www.ljmu.ac.uk/microsites/early-childhood-education-for-sustainability)
- Julie Davis on 'Australia's approach to Early Childhood Education for Sustainability'
- Arran Stibbe's (ed) book, *The Handbook of Sustainable Literacy*
- Stephen Stirling's book, *Sustainable Education: Re-Visioning Learning and Change*
- Learning through Landscapes (www.ltl.org.uk)
- International Association of Nature Pedagogy (www.naturepedagogy.com)
- Children and Nature Movement (www.childrenandnature.org)
- Permaculture Association (https://www.permaculture.org.uk)
- The OneOak project (www.sylva.org.uk/oneoak)
- Polly Higgins on 'eradicating ecocide'
- Annelies Henstra on 'children's independent right to a healthy environment, including connecting to nature'
- Claire Warden on 'nature pedagogy' and 'the International Association of Nature Pedagogy'
- The worldwide 'Permaculture' movement for developing sustainable systems of agriculture which do not harm the environment.

References and further reading

Arnold, J. C. (2014), *Their Name Is Today: Reclaiming Childhood in a Hostile World*. New York: Plough Publishing House.

Ball, D., Gill, T. & Spiegal, B. (2012). Managing Risk in Play Provision: Implementation guide [pdf]. Play England. Available at: http://www.playengland.org.uk/resources/managing-risk-in-play-provision- implementation-guide.aspx, accessed 8 August 2018.

Bath & North East Somerset Council (?). Playful Risk: Risk Benefit toolkit [pdf]. Available at: http://www.bathnes.gov.uk/sites/default/files/siteimages/Children-and-Young- People/Childcare-Play/playful_risk_-_risk_benefit.pdf, accessed 8 August 2018.

Bilton, H., Bento, G. and Dias, G. (2017) *Taking the First Steps Outside*. London: Routledge.

Carson, R. (1997), *The Sense of Wonder*. 2nd edition. New York, NY: HarperCollins.

Coster, D. & Gleeve, J. (2008). 'Give Us a Go – Children and Young People's Views on Play and Risk-taking' report [pdf]. Available at: http://www.playday.org.uk/wp-content/uploads/2015/11/give_us_a_go___children_and_young_peoples_views_on_play_and_risk_taking.pdf, accessed 8 August 2018.

Csikszentmihalyi, M. (1991), *Flow: The Psychology of Optimal Experience*. New York, NY: HarperCollins.

David, J. (ed.) (2010) *Young Children and the Environment*. Cambridge: Cambridge University Press.

Gill, T. (2012), 'When you walk or you ride or you sit or you climb, that's affordance', *Rethinking Childhood*, [blog] 30 January. Available at: https://rethinkingchildhood.com/2012/01/30/affordance/, accessed 8 August 2018.

Health and Safety Executive (2012), *Children's Play and Leisure – Promoting a Balanced Approach* [pdf]. Available at: http://www.hse.gov.uk/entertainment/childrens-play-july-2012.pdf, accessed 4 June 2018.

Herrington, S., Lesmeister, C., Nicholls, J. and Stefiuk, K. (200-). *An informational guide to young children's outdoor play spaces 7Cs*. [pdf]. Available at: http://www.wstcoast.org/playspaces/outsidecriteria/7Cs.pdf, accessed 8 August 2018.

Knight, S. (2011). *Risk and Adventure in Early Years Outdoor Play: Learning from Forest Schools*. London: SAGE.

Laevers, F. & Declercq, B. (2012). *A Process-Oriented Monitoring System for Early Years*. Belgium: CEGO Publishers.

Louv, R. (2010), *Last Child in the Woods*. London: Atlantic Books.

Louv, R. (2012), *The Nature Principle*. Chapel Hill, NC: Algonquin.

Macy, J. (2007), *World as Lover, World as Self: A Guide to Living Fully in Turbulent times*.

Macy, J. & Young Brown, M. (2014). *Coming Back to Life: The Guide to the Work that Reconnects*. Canada: New Society Publishers.

Maria Rilke, R. (2001), *The Book of Hours: Prayers to a Lowly God*, translated by Annemarie S Kidder. Evanston, IL: Northwestern University Press.

McMillan, M. (1919), *The Nursery School*. London and Toronto: J. M. Dent & Sons Ltd. California: Parallax Press.

Montessori, M. (1912), *The Montessori Method*. London: Heinemann.

Murdoch, I. (1970), *A Fairly Honourable Defeat*. Great Britain: Chatto & Windus.

Nhat Hanh, T. (1992), *Being Peace*, revised edn. Great Britain: Rider.

Nicholson, S. (1972), 'The Theory of Loose Parts: An important principle for design methodology'. *Studies in Design Education Craft & Technology*, 4(2). [online]. Available at: https://ojs.lboro.ac.uk/SDEC/article/view/1204/1171, accessed 4 June 2018.

Orr, D. W. (2004), *Earth in Mind*. Island Press.

Pelo, A. (2009), 'A pedagogy for ecology', *Rethinking Schools*. [online]. Available at: https://www.rethinkingschools.org/articles/a-pedagogy-for-ecology, accessed 4 June 2018.

Pelo, A. (2013), *The Goodness of Rain*. Redmond, WA: Exchange Press, Inc.

Pikler, E. (1940), *Peaceful Babies – Contented Mothers*. Translated from Hungarian by the Sensory Awareness Foundation. Available at: https://thepiklercollection.weebly.com/the-development-of-movement---stages.html, accessed 4 June 2018.

Play England (2015). *Practical tips for Play Rangers 2* [pdf]. Available at: http://www.playengland.org.uk/media/343457/practical-tips-for-play-rangers- 2.pdf , accessed 8 August 2018.

Possemeyer, I. (2013), 'The Touch of Memory'. *GEO*, 8. [online] Available at: http://www.traumacenter.org/products/pdf_files/memory_SMART_Warner.pdf, accessed 4 June 2018.

Roberts, R. (2010), *Wellbeing from Birth*. London: Sage.

Russell, B. (2013), *The Conquest of Happiness*, revised edn. USA: Liveright.

Solly, K. (2014) Risk, *Challenge and Adventure in the Early Years*. Abingdon, Oxon: David Fulton.

Warden, C. (2015) *Learning with Nature*. London: Sage.

White, J. (2015) *Every Child A Mover*. Watford: Early Education.

Wilson, E. O. (1986). *Biophilia* (revised edn). Cambridge, MI: Harvard University Press.

A sense of place